THE FINAL WAVE

Dismantling Patriarchy
Through Freeing Feminism

SUSANNA KRIZO

The Final Wave: Dismantling Patriarchy Through Freeing
Feminism

Revised 2020
Copyright © 2017 Susanna Krizo

ISBN-13: 978-1523769377
ISBN-10: 1523769378

Only those who are afraid of the answer
Are afraid to ask the question

Chapter 1

Learning to Make Waves

"A woman's vows I write upon the wave."

Sophocles

Waves are created when wind transfers energy to water through friction between air and water molecules. Similarly, human-made waves are created when words transfer energy to humanity through friction between opposing ideas. These human-made waves can be seen and felt in the same way as ocean waves: you can watch them from the safety of the beach or you can interact with the waves in various ways. Those who choose to stay on the beach will never understand the energy that created the waves and they may even consider the waves to be a nuisance compared to calm days. Those who choose to interact with the waves will get wet, even swept away, and it can be dangerous. But there is one thing they will never say: they will never wish the waves didn't happen.

We've had four waves of feminism in the past two hundred years, and many more that we know very little of as history has a tendency to report only the things it approves of and feminism hasn't been one of them. From the few mentions that remain we get a glimpse of a tireless effort that produced our modern world. Every generation of women, from Sappho over at Lesbos to the medieval women physicists and rebellious New England puritan women, has risen to the task in some form. Every wave has created something new, something the next generation could stand on, only to watch their efforts thwarted by the forces of patriarchy. Our generation has seen the greatest transformation due to drastic changes in politics, science, and philosophy. We are approaching a world in which all women vote,[i] and most women, although not all, have the choices that come with being in control of their own bodies and destines. Yet, not everyone thinks feminism is a good thing. Walk into a party and tell the nearest people that you are a feminist and they will look at you as if you just told them you have a communicable disease. Better yet, walk into a church and try the same and you will know what it means to be hit over the head with a Bible.[ii] Far too many see feminism as a byword, a rebellion that has gotten out of control, one that has to be ended before it takes over the whole world. Yet, if you ask the same people if women are people too—the very definition of feminism—they will give you a confused look: of course women are people too! They are just people who have children, and that makes them different, and difference means less rights for women. But when someone asks *why* the man should have more rights because he can't have children, suddenly the man is wiser of the two, and of course the wiser should rule, and everyone knows that. But why exactly is the man considered wiser?

Because the Bible says so

Even if you don't attend church or any other religious gathering, you will have heard the above phrase as God is evoked as the great Patriarch who created humanity, made the rules — including the one that says women should obey men — and wrote them down in a big book. Except God didn't. The Bible doesn't say men are wiser, or that women should obey men. It *does* say that men rule over women as a consequence of sin, but that's exactly it! People don't agree patriarchy is caused by sin. Instead they claim patriarchy is based on innate characteristics that make men and women fundamentally different. Naturally, a selective reading of any book can make it say whatever is desired; anything can be proven true when words are taken from their proper contexts — even Lucifer can be seen as a good guy, an Angel of Light. When we consider the question from this angle, we realize if male and female characteristics were truly innate and impossible to overcome, feminism wouldn't exist. In fact, patriarchal morality works hard to prevent us from following our innate needs (just think how hard abstinence advocates have to preach their message to prevent people from engaging in pre-marital sex), which is why a patriarchal theology that offers supposed innate characteristics as absolutes while suppressing actual innate characteristic creates confusion.

Due to the existing confusion, the first order of things is to find what God actually thinks about feminism and patriarchy: if God is against feminism we all need to reject it as an ungodly secular rebellion that doesn't belong in the church, or anywhere else for that matter. But if God is *for* feminism, then we have to embrace it or we'll be found fighting against God. So what exactly does God think about it?

God was the first feminist

Shocking, isn't it? It shouldn't be though, for feminism is this radical idea that women are people too, and God recognized the first woman's humanity when God called her a *female human* after her creation. But again, that's just it! We all know the first woman was a human, but that doesn't make us, or God, feminists, right? Isn't feminism about rights, or to be more precise, equal rights? It is, and it isn't. Let me explain. What is the foundation of rights? Do we have rights because we are human or are we human because we have rights? Does a baby have rights, or do we get rights as we grow older, and who decides? If we have rights because we are human, then all humans must have the same fundamental rights. If we are human because we have rights, then our humanity is decided by the amount of rights we have; the less rights, the less human we are. If the latter is true and we gain rights as we grow older, babies are less human than adults (this isn't a completely strange thought, for children's humanity is a rather recent development in human history). In other words, regardless of how we look at the argument, if women are as human as men they must have the same rights, for having less rights would make them less human. So is feminism about equal rights or not? Only if women's humanity is questioned and that is of course exactly what patriarchy does.

Patriarchy, both religious and secular, has always

considered the woman inferior to the man, but since it is no longer something that can be said out loud, not at least in the western world, we now talk about "roles." Men and women are said to have different roles: men were created to lead and women were created to marry.[iii] The glaringly obvious problem with these "roles" is the fact not every woman will marry, nor is every man a good leader. And this begs the question, what are people who don't fit within these narrow perimeters supposed to do other than pretend they are happy and well-adjusted people? In fact, when we say women are people too, but with a different role, we are essentially saying there is a difference between a person and an individual: a person has rights, an individual doesn't.

No individual human being has authority over another in his or her natural state of existence

Rights give authority, and authority gives people decision-making power over those who have fewer—or no—rights. Because of this, authority in patriarchal societies is given to people on the basis of their personhood, not their individual existence as human beings.

> In a major assessment of personhood in Africa, J.S, Fontaine has compared the concepts of personhood in four African societies. She concludes that "the completed person... is the product of a whole life. By conferring

personhood on the individual such societies also, though implicitly distinguish between person and individual, conferring moral worth not on the individual but on the social form." Fontaine's distinction between person and individual illuminates the process through which individuals attain the rights and privileges of personhood. Personhood thus carries the quality of social authority and indicates that the individual has achieved such a status. Along the way to this status, the individual gradually accrues more qualities of personhood. Marriage and having children usually play significant roles in this process, thereby entrusting the reproduction of the social unit. But personhood does not adhere evenly to men and women. Gender was historically a central part of the social construction of personhood, and in many African societies during the precolonial and colonial periods, women were considered jural minors and could not attain political office or titles, even if they could exert significant influence on kin and community.[iv]

In biblical parlance this means women were created to "help" men as their subjects, and therefore the man is a person while the woman is an individual who can sometimes become a person in a limited way.[v] This disparity was described succinctly by Augustine when he concluded the man is always in the Image of God, but the woman is in the Image of God only with the man.[vi] Theologically this belief cannot be defended, unless we say the Bible is mistaken when it says God created humanity male and female, and that this humanity is collectively in the image and likeness of God.[vii] We will shortly see how all of this played out in the English common law and what it took for women to change the laws that had made them legal nonentities. But for now, let's see if we can't find out why feminism—this idea that women are people too—is so hard to swallow for so many despite a general agreement that women are, in fact, people too.

Feminism is immoral

What did you feel when you read the above sentence? Did it make you feel good or bad? Before we talk more about it, let's look at what happens when we are faced with a decision. Our avoid-or-approach response kicks in the moment we see, hear, touch, or smell something, "That looks delicious, what is it?" "Oh, yuk, what is that smell?" We don't reason our way to those responses, rather, they appear on our mental radar whether we like it or not. Now, think of the reaction you had when you read the above sentence about feminism. Why do you think your reaction was a *feeling* rather than a rational thought? After all, the sentence didn't ask you what you *feel* about feminism; it was a statement about the morality — or, in this case, the immorality — of feminism. The answer to the question is rather simple: morals are about emotions.[viii] It may sound odd to those of us who are used to associating morals with knowledge and rational thinking, yet emotions and feelings are knowledge too, just not the reason-kind of knowledge.[ix]

Because morals are about emotional knowledge, morality isn't ruled by reason. In fact, we can sometimes have a hard time explaining rationally why we feel something is immoral or moral, and this leads us to the following conclusion:

Morals matter, but challenging morals matters more

Morals, if left unchallenged, can be based on a misguided feeling that has little to do with truth and as such can lead us to reject God's plan, and that would be immoral, wouldn't you say?

Morality, and morals in general, is a difficult subject, because it is not just about what is moral, but whether *people* are moral or not. And because morals are based on our emotions, we can get, well, emotional about the whole subject. And so, although a lot of moral arguments are in of themselves harmless, they can cause us to think *we* are moral or immoral. It is true, we can't always avoid talking about morality without implicating people since we are what we do, but we can temper our outrage with the wise words of Jesus[x]:

Judge not lest you be judged

"Judge not" doesn't mean we shouldn't make constructively critical comments (as has been pointed out *ad nauseum*), nor does being constructively critical mean we have to watch every word we say lest we hurt other people's feelings (tone policing is just another way to silence those who disagree). Judging has to do with value, declaring something to be valuable or worthless. When we judge people, we tell everyone the person in question has no value and we are therefore free to say what we want and everyone else should join in. The woman caught in adultery is the perfect example of this:

> At dawn he appeared again in the temple courts, where all the people gathered around him, and he sat down to teach them. The teachers of the law and the Pharisees brought in a woman caught in adultery. They made her stand before the group and said to Jesus, "Teacher, this woman was caught in the act of adultery. In the Law Moses commanded us to stone such

women. Now what do you say?" They were using this question as a trap, in order to have a basis for accusing him. But Jesus bent down and started to write on the ground with his finger. When they kept on questioning him, he straightened up and said to them, "Let any one of you who is without sin be the first to throw a stone at her." Again he stooped down and wrote on the ground. At this, those who heard began to go away one at a time, the older ones first, until only Jesus was left, with the woman still standing there. Jesus straightened up and asked her, "Woman, where are they? Has no one condemned you?" "No one, sir," she said. "Then neither do I condemn you," Jesus declared. "Go now and leave your life of sin."[xi]

The Pharisees wanted to trap Jesus, but Jesus couldn't be trapped, because he refused to make a value judgment. Adultery was—is—a terrible wrong, but what is worse is forgetting the value of the human being in question. The woman's value came from her origin, not her actions; actions can be amended and atoned for, but our origin will always be the same. And since we can all trace our origin to God, yet we all sin, we should follow Jesus' example and refrain from judging others, unless we want to be judged.[xii] "Do unto others what you wish them do to you" reigns supreme even when it comes to morals.

Because morals make us emotional and cause us to

judge, they cause us to have prejudices (or pre-judgments) about things and people even before we have met them. This has largely to do with *xenophobia* (fear of new people) and *misoneism* (fear of new things); the twin fears that have always plagued humanity and that have caused us to accept or reject new things and/or people.[xiii] But our decisions have also to do with how we are brought up, as emotional knowledge is something we absorb as children before we are able to use rational knowledge to weed out the worst prejudices and fears. As we grow up, these prejudices manifest themselves in ways that can be unpredictable. For example, as children we may have believed the neighbor was up to no good because of the strange smell that emanated from their kitchen every afternoon; later we learned it was Indian curry and quite delicious at that. But the question isn't just about what is strange and threatening. Morals are also about what is familiar and therefore true to us. Patriarchal ideals are considered moral because they are familiar, and they are familiar because we live in a patriarchal world and our entire intellectual framework is patriarchal.

Religion

Psychology   Mythology

Biology   **[unconscious]**   Media

Philosophy   Customs

Law

All of these institutions, belief systems, and scientific disciplines have historically said the same thing:

Religion – Women are created to serve the man, men are created to rule
Mythology – Women are created to obey, men are created to rule
Media – Women are passive objects, men are active humans
Customs – Women's sphere is the home, men's sphere is the world
Law – Women are legal minors, men are legal persons
Philosophy – Women are considered inferior, men are superior
Biology – Women are by nature inferior, men by nature superior
Psychology – Women are mentally weak, men are mentally strong

Because we are surrounded by patriarchy, our unconscious has a distinctly patriarchal bias, and we will always side with patriarchy without realizing it—unless something happens that causes us to re-evaluate.[xiv] We can call it an identity crisis or a (rude) awakening, but one day some of us find our morality isn't working for us anymore. Things that made sense yesterday, no longer makes sense; the old gives way and the new replaces the old as the norm.

It doesn't happen overnight though. Sigmund Freud's mentor, Jean-Martin Charcot, made this astute observation, "Why does the first statement of what seems a new fact always leave us cold? Because our minds have to take in something that deranges our original set of ideas, but we are all of us like that in this miserable world." Because we all tend to reject a new idea as threatening and because patriarchy claims women's subserviency is a moral question that requires a moral answer, we find feminism isn't rejected because it is rationally indefensible; it is rejected because it is emotionally reprehensible to people whose morality has been shaped by patriarchal ideals from childhood, especially because—

Morality is about getting others to agree with us

Since morality is about conformity, we tend to reject people and ideas that don't conform to our worldview. Although we can't change people's opinions, we *can* change the laws that govern our societies; we can end the man's authority using legal means and by doing so, change the underlying morality. This is why women's legal personhood with all the rights and responsibilities thereof has been and always will be one of the aims of feminism. Until the day dawns when all women are recognized as persons with equal rights, instead of subservient individuals, we must learn to make waves.

Chapter 2

"But responsibility, in its true sense, is an entirely
voluntary act; it is my response to the needs, expressed
or unexpressed, of another human being."

Erich Fromm

Morals are tricky, because we cannot give them up (moral
nihilism sounds great until we become victims of someone
else's immorality), but neither can we live by morals alone.
People who rely on morality as their sole guide tend to accept
the messages their objective unconscious provides without
questioning. It makes them more truthful than those who
ignore these messages, but their honesty is also more
misguided as the unconscious contains both good and evil
since it has accepted all kinds of information without
filtration. Reason can (for the most part) tell the difference, but
only when it is allowed to; the emotional appeal of moral
outrage is powerful and it has a tendency to turn reason off. In
addition, as no two people share the exact same moral map,
how are we going to avoid getting lost? Religious patriarchy
has a convenient answer for us—the Bible. And so we find
ourselves staring at this ancient book yet again. But before we
all turn to the Bible thinking we can find our morality there,
we need to remind ourselves (yet again) that the Bible can be

made to say a lot of things.

As with all information, we tend to look to the Bible to confirm our prior beliefs rather than allowing it to form our beliefs. Augustine recognized our confirmation bias (although he fell for it just as much as everyone else).

> Again, it often happens that a man who has attained, or thinks he has attained, to a higher grade of spiritual life, thinks that the commands given to those who are still in the lower grades are figurative; for example, if he has embraced a life of celibacy and made himself a eunuch for the kingdom of heaven's sake, he contends that the commands given in Scripture about loving and ruling a wife are not to be taken literally, but figuratively; and if he has determined to keep his virgin unmarried, he tries to put a figurative interpretation on the passage where it is said, "Marry thy daughter, and so shall thou have performed a weighty matter." ☐ Accordingly, another of our rules for understanding the Scriptures will be as follows, — to recognize that some commands are given to all in common, others to particular classes of persons, that the medicine may act not only upon the state of health as a whole, but also upon the special weakness of each member. For that which cannot be raised to a higher state must be cared for in its own state.[xv]

Since we all tend to want to confirm our prior beliefs, how can we know which text is figurative rather than prescriptive; which commands are given to all in common and which ones are given only to some or only for a given time? It is while we contemplate these things that we find that our morality is like a fog that clouds visibility until everything looks the same and good and evil become undiscernible. Revelation clears the fog enough for us to find our way out if we diligently seek it, but we must realize revelation gets us only as far as our minds allow it.

**Our eyes saw God as a distant shimmer
on the surface of the waters.
Or was it just the setting sun?**

It is important to note revelation can take many forms. It can be the astronomer gazing into the stars, or the philosopher looking for wisdom, or the theologian reading the words of the old prophets. Revelation is about that which transcends us and our world and as such it doesn't come in just one form. It could be said revelation is like the universe: it changes as we contemplate it. The one thing all revelation has in common is that its purpose is to help us re-evaluate the things we are familiar with: our world and our place in it. Revelation challenges tradition, it doesn't merely enforce it; and since reason dictates which traditions—if any—we ought to follow, an open mind is a necessity. We *must* use reason to find the truth, but since our morality tends to get in the way, we usually use our reason to justify our previous beliefs instead of challenging them. Hence we must be careful not to assign too much importance to our ability to reason; we need to also listen to the unconscious, for it contains a rich heritage of tradition that is invaluable to our human experience. In other words, we need all three—reason, tradition, and revelation— for only when they work together do we get as close as humanly possible to the truth.

As noted, morals matter, but challenging morals matters even more as morals can lead us to adopt harmful stereotypes. Unsurprisingly, we find several persistent and reoccurring stereotypes in our global moral landscape, and one of them is the belief women are emotional and men are rational. Since morals and emotions are intrinsically connected, women have been considered morally superior, and it was this belief that led the Victorians to conclude women excel in moral matters. Accordingly, women themselves believed they were morally superior to the rational man, and this perception caused them to carry the banner of *True Womanhood* proudly over their heads while they rejected the nascent women's rights movement as seen in the below response from Oberlin College.

The very idea of a woman stepping out of

"subservient wifehood" to assume a "public character" was "too unnatural to be dreamed of." On the subject of speaking in public, one of the school's female administrators wrote: "God will not lead me to speak in the assemblies because he has told me with other females, not to do so." Oberlin regarded it as its mission to show that a liberal education does not rob a woman of her nature, divest her of the softer graces and give her a masculine character." The college would be empathetically opposed to the "raving" advocates of woman's rights.[xvi]

From our perspective, it's easier to understand than it is to accept their opposition, for it is rooted in the complex web of expectations women had to contend with during the Victorian era. Not only were the Victorian women believed to be the sanctifiers of unruly men and the dispensers of religion to children (a task that required emotional acuity), they were also considered to be the sacred keepers of the home and hearth. Outside of their own sphere they were treated as trespassers in the man's world, and surprisingly most women agreed. Not that they really had a choice if they wanted to fit in, as described by Barbara Welter:

> The attributes of True Womanhood, by which a woman judged herself and was judged by her husband, her neighbors, and society, could be divided into four cardinal virtues - piety, purity,

submissiveness, and domesticity. Put them all together and the [sic] spelled mother, daughter, sister, wife – woman. Without them, no matter whether there was fame, achievement, or wealth, all was ashes. With them she was promised happiness and power.[xvii]

Victorian women represented something pure to their societies and this purity had to be protected at all cost due to the general belief women were the "second and better Eve" who would heal the world through her religious piety. At the same time scores of preachers thundered against women's rights advocates with indictments they were just like Eve who had brought ruin and despair to the world: they ought to remember their shame! Eve could be good, but only if she accepted her subordinated place in society. The first wave feminists didn't. Adding to the scandal, they talked about sex! A woman who spoke openly about sex didn't exist, or wasn't supposed to exist as her moral authority depended on her asexual nature. Naturally most women still liked the idea of sex (the "fallen woman" had to, after all, have fallen into something — or someone), but sex as a subject was considered to be a part of the man's "naughty world," a world void of the woman's purifying morality.[xviii] And so, to secure the purity of the Victorian society, society prescribed marriage and asexual domestic servanthood to all Victorian women.

There was also another reason for the prescription of religion and piety as tranquilizers for the restless women: their desire to gain political rights. The stakes must have seemed extraordinarily high for the Victorians, for in the likeness of sex, politics was considered "dirty business," and the purity of women—and therefore society—was believed to be endangered if women participated in politics. The Victorians feared what would happen if women were allowed to become legal persons with equal political rights: the very fabric of their world would be torn asunder and who knew what that would lead to; surely nothing good could come from such an event. We may shake our heads at such ideas as the granddaughters of the Victorians voted and, lo and behold, we're still here. But there was truth to their fear, a fear that was not based on reason, but on myth.[xix]

The patriarchal myth tells us men should have all authority as the ability to suppress opposition is the only justification needed to claim absolute authority.[xx] Accordingly, this myth tells us women want—or should want—what men want. Even today this myth tells us women should want what men want, and since men want power, women should allow them to have all power.[xxi] But just consider, how rational is it to insist half of humanity should obey the other half when all humans are born with a similar ability to reason? Naturally, we know myths don't follow reason; they follow the primordial instincts that hide in our collective unconscious (It is somewhat ironic we call the modern patriarchal world "civilized" as civilizations are supposedly created through the human ability to conquer its instinctual nature through rational thought). As the subjection of women cannot be defended rationally, we find the hidden truth behind the patriarchal myth to be an instinctual desire to create a power imbalance: we are told to ask ourselves why women have a problem obeying men since men have no problem obeying other men. This question can—and should—be asked also in the reverse: if men have no problem obeying other men, why do they have a problem obeying a woman?

At this point it becomes clear we are looking at a need rather than rational reasoning: men *need* women to obey them. Yet no one talks about *why* men need women to obey them; it is rather the opposite way around: w*omen* are said to need men to tell them what to do. And so we find the patriarchal myth is based on the old argument that tells us the man's rule over the woman is "for her own good."[xxii] Accordingly, those who prescribe to this myth yearn to return to a time when men ruled and women obeyed, and the world was a perfectly moral place. Not that it was exactly true, but it is the nature of myth to always portray the past in a glowing light and cause people to forget what really happened. And this in itself causes people to continue to believe the myth until something leads them to go back in time and listen to the voices from the past that tell them a very different story.

One of these voices belonged to Lucy Stone (1818-1893). She saw the reality behind the supposedly pristine Victorian society in a way that only cemented her resolve to fight the injustices and humiliations experienced by all women.

Under the terms of his will, each of his two surviving daughters was to receive $200, while his sons were to get the rest of his money and property. This was so customary that even Lucy, who knew about the will, expressed little direct resentment: "I know that Father has not done it because he loves his sons more than he does his daughters, and though there is no justice in it, still I feel it is less Father's fault than it is the fault of the time.… He probably is only acting in accordance with what he thinks is right." … However Lucy Stone might understand and condone her father's actions, it must have added to the indignation which had been building up in her since earliest childhood, an accumulation of anger over the hundreds of big and little ways in which women were constantly reminded of their inferiority. This gradual accretion of anger over one humiliation after another was a common theme in the lives of those who joined the woman's rights movement. It was something men found hard to understand. They could appreciate distress over the more glaring injustices and perhaps agree that, yes, something ought to be done about certain legal disabilities; or they might sympathize with flashes of irritation over individual slights; but they could not grasp the effect of the whole, long, abrasive process. In some women, like Lucy's mother, this process led to a steady erosion of pride and independence. In others, like Lucy herself, it built up an inflexible core of resistance, to which each humiliating incident added another firm layer.[xxiii]

Stone wasn't alone in condemning the disparity between reality and lofty morality, the ugliness created by unjust laws in a society that prided itself on its marvelous purity. Men and women, the free and the enslaved, black and white, were all keenly aware their world needed change, and most were also aware this change had to be accomplished through legal means. Lee Holcombe explains:

> In this climate of legal reform the substance of the law underwent sweeping revision. For example, the harsh criminal law was rendered more humane. The death penalty was abolished for dozens of offences and lesser punishments were instituted, while statues were enacted to protect those brought to trial for crimes—such as acts granting the accused the right to be represented by counsel, to be informed of the crown's evidence against him, to call witnesses in his behalf, and to testify in his own defence.[xxiv]

One of these unjust laws was coverture.

The common law doctrine of coverture was the law of the land in both English and American societies well into the twentieth century, although the slow dismantling began in the nineteenth century. Under this law a single woman was known as *feme sole*, a married woman was known as *feme covert*, and the law treated them differently due to their marital status.[xxv]

> To the feminists of nineteenth-century England the common law relating to the property of married women was one of the most basic, if not the most basic, of all the disabilities under which women suffered. By depriving married women of property the law deprived them of legal existence, of the rights and responsibilities of other citizens, and thus of self-respect. Since they had no property under their control, married women could not enter into contracts, nor could they sue and be sued. They could not carry on a business or trade, or could do so only with great difficulty. Married women could not be held liable for their actions, their husbands being legally responsible instead. Here the law might be as unjust to men as to women, for husbands were liable for their wives' actions whether or not they had obtained property from them. From

this it followed naturally that married women were subject to their husbands' control of their persons as well as their property. In short, the law placed married women in the same category with criminals, lunatics, and minors as being legally incompetent and irresponsible.[xxvi]

Although women had already realized their great need to obtain the vote, the dismantling of the married woman's property law was an even more urgently needed legal reform as it reduced women to legal non-entities by virtue of marriage.[xxvii] Unmarried women and widows could own property and create contracts, but married women were merged into their husbands in such a way that the two became one — and the husband was that one. Adding insult to injury, a single woman whose children were born out of wedlock had more rights to her children than a married woman, and a married woman had more rights to the personal property given to her by her friends (and even lovers!) than the property given to her by her husband. It makes no sense, but because of the law of coverture, a married woman had no separate legal existence from her husband, and without a legal existence she couldn't own anything; everything a couple owned belonged to the husband by law.

Besides property rights there was another, darker side to coverture. Because of the power imbalance, the one person who should have been the married woman's protector became all too often her enemy. An unscrupulous husband could squander away all the money (even the money earned by his wife and children), divorce his wife, marry someone else, and take the children with him. Although the church railed against divorce, the law offered almost no protection to the deserted wife. The source of the problem was the origin of the common law — the feudalistic society in which the crown expected military service from landed families — causing the man by necessity to control the land and its resources. Industrialization of society eventually reduced the amount of land owned by individuals and increased personal property, but because the law was left unchanged, the man was given absolute control of all of the couple's personal property (including his wife's wages and paraphernalia) leaving the woman with no recourses other than a reluctant court in case the man decided to forgo his duty to support the family. Equity courts provided wealthy married women a means to protect the property they had brought to the marriage, but the common law left the poorer women without a similar protection.

> Under coverture, a wife simply had no legal existence. She became, in the words of the Seneca Falls Declaration of Sentiments, "civilly dead." Any income from property she brought into the marriage was controlled by her husband, and if she earned wages outside the home, those wages belonged to him. If he contracted debts, her property went to cover his expenses. A man who killed his wife was guilty of murder and could be punished by death or

imprisonment, but a woman who killed her husband was guilty of treason against her lord and could be punished by being drawn and burnt alive. To put it most succinctly, upon marriage the husband and wife became one—him. Social norms, as reflected in the law, maintained that this was not only the natural way of things but also God's direct intent, quoting Genesis 3:16: "Your desire shall be for your husband, and he shall rule over you."[xxviii]

This one verse—Genesis 3:16—has served as the justification for the subjection of all women since the third century CE. Even people who haven't otherwise prescribed to any particular religious belief have cited this verse approvingly, and for a good reason: there is nothing more potent than "God said—" in a discussion about whether women should obey men or not.[xxix] For the Victorians, this verse was as clear as it was undisputed and only the impudent dared to disagree as seen in a conversation between Lucy Stone and her mother Hannah Stone:

> The night before Lucy was born, in 1818, Hannah milked the eight cows, since the men had gone off to save the hay from a sudden shower… She never thought of complaining. Like all the women she knew, she was doing her duty as laid down by custom and Biblical injunction. A husband was the unquestioned

head of the family; a wife did whatever she was told to do, even to milking cows at the time when she was clearly not up to it. Her rebellious little daughter felt quite differently. She had already begun to resent the authoritarian manner of her own father and of fathers in neighboring families, when she came across a statement in the Bible. "Thy desire shall be to thy husband and he shall rule over thee." This was carrying it too far. If God himself had commanded the awful subservience of women, what, she asked her mother, was the point of living, if you were a girl? Hannah Stone greatly distressed, explained the disobedience of Eve and the curse laid upon women, Hannah Stone took her Bible seriously, like many devout women of her time, she accepted her inferior and submissive role as the just punishment of the daughters of Eve. Lucy like all women must obey the words of the Bible: "Wives submit yourselves unto your husbands."[xxx]

For another hundred years, Genesis 3:16 would be the go-to verse of every patriarchal preacher and domineering husband, but the reason we talk about it in the past tense is because the unimaginable happened in the early 1990s: the verse lost its priced place as the commandment of God and was returned to its original position as a description of the man's unlawful rule over the woman. Ever since that fateful day religious patriarchy has had to defend its beliefs instead of writing the narrative as befits them, as women (who are supposed to be silent and obedient) were suddenly demanding theologians explain themselves. In the nineteenth century, however, women were still flatly ignored. Or I should say, women who obeyed were ignored. The women who sought to change existing laws were met with brutal opposition.

It didn't stop them.

To gain sympathy for their cause, women wrote fervently about the realities of life. Of being left to fend for themselves without resources, or the aid of the law in case a husband treated them cruelly, or decided to run off. Sympathetic ears heard their pleas, but not much was done until there was a general recognition the customs and laws that were in place no longer corresponded with reality—if they ever did. The defenders of coverture pointed out that the husband was legally responsible for all of the debts incurred by his wife and certainly it was a disability that caused more than one bankruptcy during the law's existence. But in general the trend went the other way, making it nearly impossible for women to protect themselves in case of divorce, desertion, or cruelty.

It was the changing economic position of

married women much more than philosophical arguments that undermined the Victorian ideal of patriarchy and led to reform of the married women's property law. Upholders of the patriarchal ideal might never be convinced by feminist arguments that marriage should represent a partnership of equals and that the family should serve as a school for democracy. But eventually they had to face the ugly fact that their principles did not coincide with practice— that there were in the country hundreds of thousands of married women who were not supported and protected by their husbands within the sheltering walls of home.[xxxi]

Just as Rosa Parks had served as an example to highlight the absurdity of segregation during the 1950s American Civil Rights Movement, the English women needed a living example to exemplify the reasons women should be recognized as legal persons, and they found one in the person of Florence Nightingale.[xxxii] Her bravery as a nurse during the Crimean War paved way for the recognition women could do extraordinary things outside of the home; purity was good and all, but practicality was better. Then there was Caroline Sheridan Norton whose misfortunes highlighted the plight of married women. Yet, neither of these two women would have called themselves feminists, and it is doubtful whether Norton would have written so much about the married women's property law had her husband not been such a rogue. Their personal low view of women in general was part of the class division that seemed to only get deeper with time: during the course of the women's rights movement, affluent women undermined the efforts of ordinary women as they had no intention to share their power and give up their privileged positon as the moral arbitrators of the Victorian society; ordinary women's responsibility was to uphold morals, not to take part in their creation.

Wealthy women weren't alone in their refusal to give up their power. Privilege and human rights clashed in factories and on the street as people demanded improved working conditions through strikes and riots.[xxxiii] People were mobilizing, and women, although ridiculed as unfeminine, had no intention to miss the opportunity to free themselves. In the absence of leadership from Nightingale and Norton, the organizing of the women's rights movement in England was left to Barbara Leigh Smith and her fiery feminist friends. Smith was a radical in every way, and her financial independence allowed her to break the norms of her society without having to fear financial repercussions. And this leads us to an important conclusion: patriarchy isn't inevitable; it's artificial and maintained through wealth.[xxxiv]

Financial independence dismantles patriarchy

The first step towards freedom was the Divorce Act of 1857. Unfortunately the law improved only the circumstances of women who were deserted and otherwise cruelly treated, but it did nothing to help the women who were still married. Finally in 1870, fourteen years since its original presentation to the English parliament, the married women's property law was removed from the law books and married women could once again own property and keep the wages from their own work. But there was still no law that recognized women's full personhood. The elective franchise (the vote), for example, would come decades later after many arduous years of campaigning, protesting, and agitating, and women were once again its most ardent opponents.

One of the great enigmas of patriarchy is why women are in some ways their own greatest enemies as far as equal rights are concerned. Instead of uniting, women fight. Homemakers and working women side-eye each other, wealthy women reject financial reform, and poor women turn a blind eye to racism and discrimination if it gives them economic advantage. All of this is done with ostensibly good intention, but intentions can also lead us astray as Cicero pointed out, "Crimes are not measured by the issue of events, but from the bad intentions of men." Intentions can take us to a lot of places, but they rarely take us where we need to be. When it comes to morals and intentions we seek to get what we want regardless of whether it is good or bad and we're spectacularly good at justifying our decisions. Women aren't any better than men in this respect, for also women vie for a higher place in the hierarchy. And so we find women will argue against the legal personhood of all women if it secures their *own* position, and religious women tend to lean toward *less rights* as they have a very distinct role within their own communities as the feminine voice of patriarchy that is designed to keep other women (especially those outside of their own communities) in their proper place.

It is of course worth noting religion can be a great catalyst toward freedom. Faith was the inspiration of more than one person who took on religious patriarchy in the nineteenth century in an effort to liberate others. The Quakers were the first to condemn slave-owning by Christians after the church decided slavery and Christianity were compatible in 1667.[xxxv] They were also the first to publicly condemn the forced subjection of women in all spheres of life. The subject matter itself was nothing new. It had been talked about for decades, even centuries, but what was new was the fervor with which Christians went after what they believed were injustices perpetuated upon humankind; the same fervor that had been felt by early Christians when they witnessed the injustices of the Roman world. And it is only natural as liberation is found in all systems that replace an egocentric view with a holistic view of life.

An egocentric view sees salvation as a destiny, a way for an individual to escape this life. The here-and-now loses its meaning, and salvation becomes about "saving souls," not about saving bodies and minds from exploitation. And yet, salvation isn't found outside of life; salvation *is* life. From Exodus to the Cross, God has called humanity to set the oppressed and enslaved free. It was the message of the prophets and apostles alike, and it is the rallying cry of our time as well as the Kingdom of God doesn't grow when people are subjected to control; it grows when people are set free.

> Instead, speaking the truth in love, we will grow to become in every respect the mature body of him who is the head, that is, Christ. From him the whole body, joined and held together by every supporting ligament, grows and builds itself up in love, as each part does its work.[xxxvi]

The patriarchal boat rocked on the waves created by feminism for decades. And just as any boat that keeps on taking in water until it sinks, in the early decades of the twentieth century *True Womanhood* gave way to the *New Woman* in a glorious display of equality. But only a couple decades later, patriarchy found a way to quell the progress and the post-WWII well-educated voting woman found herself holding on to the dream of a life outside of the home, tying an apron with one hand while holding a baby with the other. Despite all the advancements in women's rights, the "Feminine Mystique" as Betty Friedan so aptly named it, ensured women's legal personhood did nothing for them as long as they weren't able to control how many children they had. And so women embraced the cult of domesticity all over again and cleaned their homes until their hands were white from the bleach, hoping something would happen that would change their lives.

In the meanwhile, the battle for equal rights continued unabated. The Equal Rights Amendment (ERA) was introduced in US Congress in 1923, three years after the Nineteenth Amendment was ratified. The ERA was passed in 1972, but failed to be ratified by the individual states (only three more were needed). This abysmal turn of events has been attributed to the efforts of one woman whose singlehanded determination caused the amendment's defeat—Phyllis Schlafly. Schlafly wasn't an unlikely candidate. Married into wealth, and having failed to secure a political career for herself, Schlafly made a name for herself through STOP ERA, "stop" being an acronym for "Stop Taking Our Privileges" (the privileges being separate bathrooms and alimony). Similarly to her wealthy Victorian counterparts, Schlafly advocated for strong family values, and the rejection of communism. But although patriarchy had found in Schlafly a woman who would fight for the cult of domesticity while living like a feminist, the tide couldn't be completely reversed. Without flinching, the second wave tackled the larger questions of nature versus humanity, women versus the kitchen. The newly created contraceptives gave women new choices, and women joined the larger world in ever-growing numbers. The future was bright! But then a large cloud appeared on the horizon as religious patriarchy resurrected itself from the ashes.

The influence of religious patriarchy diminished steadily after women became legal persons in the twentieth century, and the final nail in its coffin was the near universal agreement Genesis 3:16 wasn't God's commandment. And yet, the adherents of religious patriarchy refused to accept defeat without putting up a fight. In 1985 the former feminist Mary Pride published "A Way Home: Beyond Feminism, Back to Reality"; a book that would serve as the impetus for the Quiverfull movement and the Christian Patriarchy movement (Pride doesn't like to take credit for this influence). The conservative egalitarian organization, *Christians for Biblical Equality* (CBE), was created in 1987 as a response to the affirmation of same sex love by the *Ecumenical Evangelical Women's Caucus* (EEWC). A few years later, in 1989, the patriarchal organization, *The Council on Biblical Manhood and Womanhood* (CBMW), was created as a response to CBE. In 1997 Joshua Harris wrote "I Kissed Dating Goodbye," teaching an entire generation about courtship and abstinence. But the show got really going in 1998 when *Vision Forum* was formed under the leadership of Doug Phillips promoting homeschooling and the Quiverfull lifestyle (a program that went sour after legal actions were filed against him).[xxxvii] As if all of the above wasn't enough, the patriarchal *pièces de résistance* came in 2004 in the form of "Created to Be His Help Meet" by Debi Pearl, a book designed to teach women how to properly obey their husbands. While the rest of the world was largely unaware of what was going on behind closed doors, in 2010 Kathryn Joyce published "Quiverfull: Inside the Christian Patriarchy Movement," exposing the Christian patriarchal world for all to see. We're still dealing with the aftermath, and we will for many years to come. Nevertheless, the return of religious patriarchy shouldn't come as a surprise to anyone as one of the reasons patriarchal ideology is able to reproduce itself in every generation is its ability to lodge itself into the very core of our lives, our human institutions; and religion is just one of them.

Chapter 3

The Crucible

"An unjust situation does not happen by chance;
It is not something branded by a fatal destiny:
There is human responsibility behind it."

Gustavo Gutierrez

The home is the crucible where patriarchal ideology is lived and experienced by everyone. With the return of religious patriarchy at the end of the twentieth century there was a noted increase in beliefs and practices that emphasized the man's authority in the home. Two concepts—primogeniture and "covering"—were used to sidetrack revelation to create the same conditions in the modern home and church as coverture created in all society during the Victorian era. The first concept, primogeniture, dictates the way inheritance is shared: the eldest son inherits all of the father's property and goods; daughters are given some money and are guided to (hopefully) marry the men who inherit. When primogeniture is inserted into theology and combined with the (presumed) greater wisdom of the man, the first man's prior creation makes the man the ruler of all creation (as the heir of God) and the woman is seen as created to marry, serve, and obey the man.[xxxviii] She exists as an appendage to the man and her role as the man's "helper" requires her perfect merging with

the man until her own self vanishes — just as in coverture.[xxxix]
Unsurprisingly, we find the second theological concept, "covering," supplementing primogeniture by providing the reason why the woman must be deprived of all independence: a woman must be "covered" by a man's authority at all times; a belief that comes straight from the old English common law, as described by William Blackstone in 1765:

> By marriage, the husband and wife are one person in law: that is, the very being or legal existence of the woman is suspended during the marriage, or at least is incorporated and consolidated into that of the husband; *under whose wing, protection, and cover, she performs everything;* and is therefore called in our law-French a feme-covert, femina viro co-operta; is said to be covert-baron, or under the protection and influence of her husband, her baron, or lord; and her condition during her marriage is called her coverture. Upon this principle, of a union of person in husband and wife, depend almost all the legal rights, duties, and disabilities, that either of them acquire by the marriage.[xl]

In the likeness of their Victorian counterparts, modern Christian women aren't allowed to vote in churches governed by elders, nor are they allowed to speak from the pulpit or have authority over a man, as they aren't considered full members of the Body of Christ. They are half-members just as their great-grandmothers were half-members of their own societies, lumped together with infants, criminals, and the feebleminded, under someone else's authority "for their own good."[xli]

Coverture isn't the only way religious and secular patriarchy mesh in the intellectual realm. Inequality between men and women is a common theme in all patriarchal literature. Aristotle wrote in *Nicomachean Ethics* about friends, how they must always reciprocate goodwill and treat each other as equals; a good man doesn't use his friends, nor does he consider them inferior to himself.[xlii] Yet, according his other work, *Politics,* between a man and a woman inequality is permanent.[xliii] Similarly, we find our modern theologians insisting all humans are created equal according to Genesis 1 (the Image of God is found in everyone), but the woman is the man's subject because of Genesis 2 (she was created to "help" the man). Theologians use the same logic as Aristotle with the same intended end-result: friendship and equality are reserved for men; women exist to serve men.

Property has always been at the heart of the inequality that exists between men and women. The ancient Greeks understood this just as perfectly as the English Victorians:

> When a man owns inheritable property, he must own a wife too, in order to ensure a legitimate heir. The fact that women are private wives entails that in many ways they are treated as property rather than as persons. They themselves cannot inherit real property, which

to a large extent defines personhood with the society (a disinherited son must leave the city unless another citizen adopts him as his heir); and they are treated as commodities to be given away by their male relatives. With these as the basic features of the social structures of the city, it is not surprising that Plato, in spite of general pronouncements to the contrary, is not able to treat women as the equals of his male citizens. Their status as property seems to prevent the execution of his declared intentions.[xliv]

When property ownership makes us legal persons, women cannot own property and remain subjects at the same time. Hence, to prevent the woman's equality with the man, the woman has been denied both land and political rights. This last thought brings us back to the old law of coverture as it is here the feudal origin of coverture finds its clearest manifestation. The feudal laws vested the local lords with judicial power in their own domains before the invention of courts. The King was the ultimate sovereign and lord who owned all lands and granted land to his vassals in exchange of military service. The king's vassals (the lords) granted the right of use of land to their own vassals, creating a complicated hierarchy of authority and responsibility. Because men had to render military service to the king, the land was by necessity controlled by the man. This was the arrangement that became the foundation for the laws of coverture that made the man the woman's lord and the woman the man's "serf." The woman had the responsibility to perform manual work and maintain the household, but not the right to own property or have any say in its management. Unable to own property under coverture, the woman's existence depended solely on the goodwill of the man just as the existence of the landless feudal serfs had depended on the goodwill of their feudal lords.

Until the nineteenth century only landowners were allowed to vote, but eventually the vote was given to all men. The inclusion of all men (whether they owned land or not) into the elective franchise made the exclusion of women such a glaring example of all the injustices heaped upon women, the women decided they had to secure the vote for themselves. Securing the vote could have been far more straightforward if money hadn't been in the way in every way. As already noted, the members of the wealthy upper class weren't willing to lose the privileges that came with their social position. As a result, there were attempts to restrict women's voting due to fears that middleclass men, whose numbers were greater than those of upper class men, would attempt to coerce their wives to vote for their own candidate (giving each man effectually two votes). But some went so far as to exclude even adult men in order to prevent married men with children from having more than one vote. For example, the political philosopher, James Mill, excluded all women, children, *and* adult men under forty as their interests were considered already to be involved in those of their fathers and husbands. Jeremy Bentham disagreed as he believed all adults should be allowed to vote, but he nevertheless excluded women and gave final say (and the vote) to the husbands on the basis of their greater physical strength, "hoping" they would consider the interests of their wives—at least occasionally.[xlv]

And they wonder why women revolted.

Mill's son, John Stuart Mill saw the inherent contradictions in his father's arguments and set out to end the man's authority in the home and society at large. In his book, "The Subjection of Women," he argued against the laws he believed were unjust, seeking a way to end the injustices by reforming the philosophy behind the law of coverture.

> If they mean what they say, their opinion must evidently be that men do not render the married conditions so desirable to women, as to induce them to accept it for its own recommendations. It is not a sign of one's thinking the boon one offers very attractive, when one allows only Hobson's choice, "that or none." And here, I believe, is the clue to the feelings of those men, who have a real antipathy to the equal freedom of women. I believe they are afraid, not lest women should be unwilling to marry, for I do not think that any one in reality has that apprehension; but lest they should insist that marriage should be on equal conditions; lest all women of spirit and capacity should prefer doing almost anything else, not in their own eyes degrading, rather than marry, when marrying is giving themselves

a master, and a master too of all their earthly
possessions.[xlvi]

Equality and equal participation in all realms of life was Mill's
cure to the ills he had observed. Had he lived long enough to
see how far we've come in a century and a half, he would
most certainly have felt vindicated and rightly so; modern
women expect equality. Unfortunately, marriages that deprive
women from their personhood in the likeness of coverture do
still exist all around the world, even in societies that uphold
equality by law. It is in itself an issue that needs to be
addressed as the infantilizing of women is done deliberately
in order to foster docility. The reason behind the forced
docility is the simple fact that without marriage the
patriarchal home wouldn't exist; without the patriarchal home
the man wouldn't have authority over women, and without
the man's authority there would be no patriarchy. Mill was
right about that one.

Feminism's *fait accompli* of overturning coverture and the
married woman's property law was not well received by the
adherents of patriarchy, and it was only to be expected as the
home is the crucible of patriarchal authority. Patriarchal
societies have always understood this, which is why men have
been willing to share authority with women outside the home

(albeit grudgingly and only in limited ways), but in the home every man has asserted his authority over his wife and children. There is a perfectly logical reason for this: if a man doesn't have authority in the home, the man's authority in all other realms of life cannot be defended. This truth is rarely mentioned, yet it is always found in the background as seen in a discussion about women's ordination that was held at the Methodist Protestant Conference in New York in 1880 where Anna Howard Shaw was questioned about her desire to be ordained.

> "Paul said, Wives, obey your husbands," shouted my old man of the coat-tails. "Suppose your husband should refuse to allow you to preach? What then?"
> "In the first place, "I answered, "Paul did not say so, according to the Scriptures. But even if he did, it would not concern me, for I am a spinster."
> The old man looked me over "You might marry some day," he predicted, cautiously.
> "Possibly," I admitted. "Wiser women than I am have married. But is equally possible that I might marry a man who would command me to preach; and in that case I want to be all ready to obey him."[xlvii]

This rather humorous exchange reveals the heart of the problem: if the man has authority in the home, a woman is under that authority in all other realms of life as well, even in the church. Or I should say, *especially* in the church, for although coverture as a legal doctrine was abolished in the twentieth century, the same old argument is still found in theology. And it's only to be expected as religious patriarchy gave coverture some of its earliest shape; and all patriarchy, whether secular or religious, has the same general goal—to give the man authority over the woman.

The Victorians believed the man's authority in the home was a God-given right everyman enjoyed, but there was also another more peculiar reasoning behind the law itself:

> The disabilities attached to infancy are designed as a protection, for the inexperienced, against the fraudulent; those incident to coverture, are the simple consequence of that sole authority which the law has recognized in the husband, subject to judicial interference whenever he transgresses its proper limits. In that variety of wills with which human nature is ordinarily constituted, it is absolutely necessary for the preservation of peace, that where two or more persons are destined to pass their lives together, one should be endued with such a pre-eminence as may

prevent or terminate all contestation. And why is this pre-eminence exclusively vested in the man? — Simply, because he is the stronger.[xlviii]

Because of the man's greater physical strength a married woman had to give up her own individual existence as the Victorians feared what the man would do if a woman was given equality, or (horror of all horrors!) authority over him.

In his hands the power allotted him at once supports itself without external interference; give but the legal authority to the wife, and every moment would produce a revolt on the part of the husband, only to be quelled by assistance from without. Nor is this the only reason: it is always probable that the man, by his education and manner of life, has acquired more experience, more aptitude for business, and a greater depth of judgment than the woman. In both these respects there are sometimes exceptions but the ordinary course of things must be that kept in view by the law. They who, from some ill-defined notion of justice or generosity, would extend to women an absolute equality, hold out to them a dangerous snare. Let the law by conferring equality on wives, once release them from that necessity of pleasing which is at present imposed up on them and it would in fact, instead of strengthening, only subvert the empire they now enjoy. Man forgets his self-love while secure of his prerogative, and derives enjoyment even from concession: substitute for the relation in which he now stands, a jealousy of rival power, and the continually wounded pride of the stronger party would soon rouse up in him a dangerous antagonist for the weaker; he would regard rather what he had lost than what he retained; and would turn all his efforts to the forcible establishment of that prerogative which is now subdued by the dominion of female influence.[xlix]

For the Victorian mind equality was an utter impossibility due to the simple fact that if women didn't find it necessary to please their husbands, the men would turn to selfishness and violence; although husbands could always resort to selfishness and violence if they felt slighted, making the point rather moot. But although general agreement affirmed one person should have all authority in the home, even the Victorians couldn't exactly explain why it had to be the man.

[Footnote (b)] It is hoped that the preceding consideration of the true grounds of marital authority, may not be deemed altogether useless or 'misplaced; as it is only by an accurate conception of the reason of the law, that we can ever argue consistently on the law itself. — Mr. Fonblanque, in his note to Eq. Tr. 9, considers the disabilities imposed on married women to rest on this — "that if they were not allowed to bind their husbands, they might, by the abuse of such a power, involve their husbands and families in ruin." It might be so while the husband also possesses unlimited power of charging his own estate, which could never- be large enough to satisfy the demands of too [sic], if by chance they disagreed. This hypothesis, therefore, only shews the policy of vesting a sole authority in one; but it does not explain why that one should be the man.[1]

Despite their qualms, the Victorians didn't miss an opportunity to defend the man's authority in the home, and women were just as passionate in their efforts. But the lack of a justifiable reason for vesting the man with all power proved detrimental to their cause. This is revealed rather candidly in a private correspondence between a husband and wife from the eighteenth century, before the dismantling of coverture began in all earnest.

Abigail Adams sent a letter to her husband John in which she asked him to "remember the ladies" in the new code of laws.

March 31, 1776
Abigail Adams to John Adams

… I long to hear that you have declared an

independency. And, by the way, in the new code of laws which I suppose it will be necessary for you to make, I desire you would remember the ladies and be more generous and favorable to them than your ancestors. Do not put such unlimited power into the hands of the husbands. Remember, all men would be tyrants if they could. If particular care and attention is not paid to the ladies, we are determined to foment a rebellion, and will not hold ourselves bound by any laws in which we have no voice or representation. That your sex are naturally tyrannical is a truth so thoroughly established as to admit of no dispute; but such of you as wish to be happy willingly give up -- the harsh tide of master for the more tender and endearing one of friend. Why, then, not put it out of the power of the vicious and the lawless to use us with cruelty and indignity with impunity? Men of sense in all ages abhor those customs which treat us only as the (servants) of your sex; regard us then as being placed by Providence under your protection, and in imitation of the Supreme Being make use of that power only for our happiness....

April 14, 1776
John Adams to Abigail Adams

... As to your extraordinary code of laws, I

cannot but laugh. We have been told that our struggle has loosened the bonds of government everywhere; that children and apprentices were disobedient; that schools and colleges were grown turbulent; that Indians slighted their guardians, and negroes grew insolent to their masters. But your letter was the first intimation that another tribe, more numerous and powerful than all the rest, were grown discontented. This is rather too coarse a compliment, but you are so saucy, I won't blot it out. Depend upon it, we know better than to repeal our masculine systems. Although they are in full force, you know they are little more than theory. We dare not exert our power in its full latitude. We are obliged to go fair and softly, and, in practice, you know we are the subjects. We have only the name of masters, and rather than give up this, which would completely subject us to the despotism of the petticoat, I hope General Washington and all our brave heroes would fight....

May 7, 1776
Abigail Adams to John Adams

... I cannot say that I think you are very generous to the ladies; for, whilst you are proclaiming peace and good-will to men,

emancipating all nations, you insist upon
retaining an absolute power over wives. But you
must remember that arbitrary power is like most
other things which are very hard, very liable to
be broken; and, notwithstanding all your wise
laws and maxims, we have it in our power, not
only to free ourselves, but to subdue our
masters, and without violence, throw both your
natural and legal authority at our feet....[li]

Whereas Ms. Adams saw with clarity the future rebellion, Mr. Adams refused to consider any change to existing laws. What makes his refusal rather galling was his own attitude when he found himself sidelined:

Adams' two terms as Vice President were
frustrating experiences for a man of his vigor,
intellect, and vanity. He complained to his wife
Abigail, "My country has in its wisdom
contrived for me the most insignificant office
that ever the invention of man contrived or his
imagination conceived."[lii]

Despite his own unhappiness, he was all too happy to condemn *all* women to permanent insignificancy due to the "wisdom" of men.

From the above brief exchange an important detail emerges: men and women did not perceive the law of coverture in the same way. Ms. Adams called it "tyranny";

Mr. Adams called it a "masculine system." And as Ms. Adams pointed out, and he himself affirmed, Mr. Adams believed rebellion against tyrants was obedience to God, although for some peculiar reason he seemed to have thought it applied only to freeborn men.[liii] We see this same attitude even in our day: while theologians talk about the "office" of the husband, modern women talk about the "oppressive" husband. Transforming the man's authority into something impersonal, something the man must reluctantly accept—"God insists, not I, dear"—can make it easier to swallow even when it cannot be entirely justified. Yet, if the man's rule must be made impersonal, isn't it evidence that in the personal realm the man's authority is as unnatural as it is unwelcomed due to its impersonal nature? In the end it all comes down to power—personal power. Even during coverture the impersonal law faded into the background while the very real person of the husband took center stage with all of his preferences and idiosyncrasies; it was the husband's word that became law in the home—and with it came the tyranny Ms. Adams wanted to see abolished.[liv] And there was a reason for it: parenting.

The Greek *oikos* (household) was an economic unit: the union of a man and a woman, together with the peculiar institution of slavery, made life possible in a world void of automation. Ever since the abolition of slavery and the industrial revolution, our homes have been transformed into miniature daycare centers—nothing much beyond the nurture of children happens in our homes during the day. And this leads us to the often concealed truth: the modern nuclear family is designed to perpetuate the myth parenting is women's work as the mother ostensibly obeys the child, and men (who expect to be obeyed) couldn't possibly be asked to obey a child.

Chapter 4

Biology and Mothering

"Motherhood is neither a duty nor a privilege,
But simply the way that humanity can satisfy the desire
For physical immortality and triumph over the fear of death."

Rebecca West

Twenty-five hundred years ago the Athenian philosopher Aristotle wrote:

> As in other departments of science, so in politics, the compound should always be resolved into the simple elements or least parts of the whole. We must therefore look at the elements of which the state is composed, in order that we may see in what the different kinds of rule differ from one another, and whether any scientific result can be attained about each one of them. He thus considers things in their first growth and origin, whether a state or anything else, will obtain the clearest view of them. In the first place there must be a union of those who cannot exist without each other; namely, of male and female, that the race may continue (and this is a union which is formed, not of deliberate purpose, but

because, in common with other animals and with plants, mankind have a natural desire to leave behind them an image of themselves), and of natural ruler and subject, that both may be preserved. For that which can foresee by the exercise of mind is by nature intended to be lord and master, and that which can with its body give effect to such foresight is a subject, and by nature a slave; hence master and slave have the same interest. Now nature has distinguished between the female and the slave. For she is not niggardly, like the smith who fashions the Delphian knife for many uses; she makes each things for a single use, and every instrument is best when intended for one and not for many uses. But among barbarians no distinction is made between women and slaves, because there is no natural ruler among them: they are a community of slaves, male and female. Wherefore the poets say—'It is meet that Hellenes should rule over barbarians'; as if they thought that the barbarian and the slave were nature one. Out of these two relationships between man and woman, master and slave, the first thing to arise is family, and Hesiod is right when he says—'First house and wife and an ox for the plough', for the ox is the poor man's slave.[lv]

According to Aristotle, men and women come together to fulfill their biological instinct to perpetuate their species. But because this coming together would imply sexual equality he had to amend his conclusion by saying some are born to rule and that also *this* distinction is biological. Aristotle offered a functional explanation as proof: according to his philosophy we are all born to perform a function, and this function is determined by one's ability to reason.[lvi]

   a) The man's superior rational mind makes him the ruler.
   b) The woman's reason lacks authority, restricting her role to childbearing and management of the household.
   c) Children's reason is immature, their role is to study.
   d) Slaves lack a deliberative faculty entirely, making them living tools in the hands of a master.

Aristotle's explanation was based on what he believed was the basic relationship of the mind to the body: the greater the ability to reason, the greater that person's position in both home and public, and lesser the burden to maintain the physical body and its needs. As a result of this distinction, Aristotle considered marriage between a freeborn man and a freeborn woman to be the only legitimate way to create a household (*oikos*) as households in turn formed the state (*polis*) that allowed some to engage in a political life. All of this begs naturally the question, who was allowed to engage in this political life? According to Aristotle, only those whose reason was perfected—i.e., freeborn men—were allowed to make decisions in *Ekklēsia,* the political assembly of Athens; women and slaves were responsible for the maintenance of the physical body in *oikos*.

The reason Aristotle's model was primarily concerned with functionality (women's only function in life was to have children and obey their husbands) was his wish to exclude women from decision making. We can't, of course, blame Aristotle for arguing for something every man has considered his birth right. His enduring success lies largely in his ability to put into words what most men have always thought. Accordingly, when he argued the woman's reason lacks authority, he was describing everyman's reluctance to allow a woman influence his thoughts and actions — a man should be free to make his own deliberations without the interference of a woman.

> It seems, then, as has been said, that man is a moving principle of actions; now deliberation is about the things to be done by the agent himself, and action are for the sake of things other than themselves.... If we are to always be deliberating, we shall have to go on to infinity. For every one ceases to inquire how he is to act when he has brought the moving principle back to himself and to the ruling part of himself; for this is what chooses. This is plain also from the ancient constitutions, which Homer presented; for the kings announced their choices to the people. The object of choice being one of the things in our own power which is desired after

deliberation, choice will deliberate desire of things in our own power; for when we have decided as a result of deliberation, we desire in accordance with our deliberation.[lvii]

In words everyone can understand, a woman's reason must be without authority or she would have to be allowed to act as a result of her own deliberation, and that would also mean women would by necessity have the right to tell a man what to do on occasion. By removing the right from the woman to deliberate and act according to her own deliberation, Aristotle placed her squarely under the man's authority and history would leave her there for more than two millennia, until science finally liberated her. But before that blessed event took place, as philosophy's influence was waning, nineteenth-century science became patriarchy's new tool in the effort to keep women subjected to the man's authority.

Charles Darwin rejected Aristotle's teleological (functional) explanation as he was convinced functionality had little to do with the evolution of a particular feature that enabled life to evolve. Instead of assigning a function to lifeforms, Darwin recognized there were variations within species and that not every lifeform was meant to evolve to a higher form or be perfected; bacterium is still needed as is. But this brings us to two questions: why did Darwin believe the man evolved differently compared to the woman, and why did he believe the difference automatically gave the man an evolutionary advantage over the woman?

In the early days of evolutionary theory, the man was believed to be more rational due to his larger brain size, a belief that makes the blue whale the wisest of all mammals. As the premise was somewhat difficult to defend (for obvious reasons) Darwin brought also up the persistent argument women have never made any significant contributions to science, philosophy, or the arts. Had Darwin looked a bit closer at the history he was boasting about he may have changed his mind:

> His [Plato] disciples were Speusippus of Athens, Xenocrates of Chalcedon, Aristotle of Stagira, Philippus of Opus, Hestiaeus of Perinthus, Dion of Syracuse, Amyclus of Heraclea, Erastus and Coriscus of Scepsus, Timolaus of Cyzicus, Euaon of Lampsacus, Python and Heraclides of Aenus, Hippothales and Callipus of Athens, Demetrius of Amphipolis, Heraclides of Pontus, and many others, **among them two women,** Lastheniea of Mantinea and Lasthenia of Phlius who is reported by Dicaearchus to have worn men's clothes).[lviii]

Since Darwin focused on the apparent differences between men and women, and because he believed a singular cause explained the origin of all life, he had to find the mechanism that had formed two *kinds* of humans out of the original amoeba. He found a plausible explanation in sexual selection.

> Darwin concluded that some traits were due to sexual selection. These included hairlessness on the human torso and limbs, and the numerous other secondary sexual characteristics which differentiate humans from all other animals. What remains unanswered is why males or females would select certain traits in a mate when they had been successfully mating without them for eons and when most primates did not prefer these traits. Unfortunately, in this case, "Darwin, as usual, looked for a single cause to explain all of the facts." If sexual selection caused the development of a male beard and its lack on females, why do so many women prefer shaven males? Obviously, culture is critical in what is considered sexually attractive. These standards change greatly, precluding the long term sexual selection needed to develop them biologically.[lix]

Since (patriarchal) culture had created the traits Darwin observed, it shouldn't come as a surprise to find Darwin arguing *men* decide what is desirable in women.

> Further, Darwin attributed most female traits to male sexual selection, but only a few male traits

to female selection. He felt that females were not fussy about their mate's physical appearances. Therefore, males were not only "more powerful in body and mind than women" but had even "gained the power of selection" - evolution was in the males' hands, and females were largely passive. Women, consequently, were less evolved and more primitive; this is why instinct and emotions dominated women, a fact which was her "greatest weakness."[lx]

The emotional woman makes an entrance yet again, but this time her emotional nature makes her morally weaker, rather than stronger, than the man. Accordingly, we find Darwin concluding female inferiority was the major proof sexual selection had created some of our distinct, yet differentiated, human traits. But if Darwin was right and men have molded women for centuries we should by now find only the inferior, docile, obedient women all men look for, and the feminist movement should be a biological impossibility. Tellingly, Darwin himself complained that "unchecked female militancy threatened to produce a perturbance of the races and to divert the orderly process of evolution." As with most, if not all patriarchal thought, the truth is found in the exact opposite direction: more recent research tells us sexual selection is *run by women* as women are far more pragmatic in their mate selection than men. This thought was already know during Darwin's time, but it was too much for the Victorians who couldn't fathom a world in which women had more say than men. And so we find, although patriarchy claims its ideology is according to nature, it actually hinders sexual selection. And by hindering sexual selection patriarchy prevents the further evolution of the human species; which is perhaps the reason why the saying, "History repeats itself," has become such a maxim.

Once the inferiority of women was finally set aside as biologists agreed women run sexual selection, the idea women are destined to become mothers at the exclusion of all other opportunities lost much of its previous halo. But it created another more acute problem—the rejection of motherhood. Because feminism has had to fight a double battle of affirming motherhood while resisting the idea of motherhood being the only role available for women, feminism has become linked to the belief motherhood is somehow a lesser role. And yet, the denigration of motherhood is in itself part and parcel of patriarchal thought.

The original *coup de grâce* of patriarchy was its success in transforming childbirth from a gloriously wonderful and natural process into something shameful and disgusting. From menstruation to menopause, women themselves have become convinced there is something wrong with them, and that children are something they must give to the world in return for being in some ways defective. Childbirth itself is considered shameful largely because it is something only women can do; killing people is considered honorable because it is what men do. Accordingly, in patriarchal theology God is portrayed as an angry father who kills instead of a tender mother who nurtures, and **Chung Hyun Kyung didn't miss the reason for it:**

> Many Asian women think God as a life-giving power can be naturally personified as mother and woman because woman gives birth to her children and her family members by nurturing them. In many Asian women's writings, God is portrayed as mother and woman. Some Asian women claim that women are more sensitive to fostering life than men because of women's experience of giving birth and nurturing others. A group of Asian women emphasized the point by reflecting on the event of Moses' birth and killing of males infants in Exodus: *"Every woman is close to life and loves her child. Woman is life and love. The killing of the male baby is ironic of the two edged sword that patriarchy has in itself, namely, in male power is also death."* God as mother and woman challenges the old concept that emphasized, along with other attributes, God as immutable and unchangeable. Women's body grows and changes radically through menstruation and pregnancy compared to the male body. God as mother is more approachable

and personable. When Asian women begin to image God as woman and mother, they also being to accept their own bodies and their own womanhood in its fullest. The female God accepts us as we are more than the patriarchal male God.[lxi]

When God is seen as a mother, women's humanity and motherhood are affirmed as both natural and supranatural events: women exist through God's creative work, and humans exist through women's creative work. It is through this work we can tell creation is good, that *we* are good. And because of this inherent goodness, motherhood should be celebrated by all women as a unique and priceless contribution only they can give to the world. Yet, although motherhood is a unique gift, it is an individual gift; it is not a mandate. Women don't *have* to have children. If they decide to have children, the children are *their* children. Just consider, how many of us would agree to be forced to accept a job against our wishes and abilities? It is what is done to women all around the world when they are told motherhood is the *only* choice. Children are a blessing, but so is every opportunity out there.

Motherhood would have elevated women, if men hadn't

decided their own ability to take life was far more important than women's ability to give life, and the reason for it can be described with one word—envy. Womb envy has caused men to denigrate women instead of valuing them as equal partners in life. We see this in every culture where women are devalued, and it's especially true of cultures where religion is one of the main sources of the oppression.

To hide women's unique ability to give life, the asexual Christian God was transformed into a vengeful male god who creates without the female principle and destroys those who disobey. The complete exclusion of women from the primordial creation has created a vacuum in theology: where do women fit in the grand scheme of things? What purpose do women serve here on earth? Do they themselves create life, or are they only vessels for the man's creative impulse? If women are only vessels, the children aren't really theirs to begin with. Traditionally children have always belonged to the father for this very reason; only recently have mothers gained rights to their own children. Naturally the pendulum swung quickly to the other extreme when women began to gain political rights: we now believe children who are deprived of their mothers even for a moment will suffer. And so the women, who in previous centuries feared divorce because it would automatically mean the loss of their children, came to find anything beyond fulltime mothering causes people to view them as "bad mothers"—an extremely negative term that comes with the worst kind of moral censure; the only good kind of mother is the kind that is always home.

To add insult to injury, although mothers are now seen

as pure and saintly (as long as they are *only* mothers), we continue to speak of our primordial mothers as if they were the cause of the ruin of all humankind: both Eve and Pandora are considered cursed as they are said to have brought evil to the world. This belief was created to enforce the part of the patriarchal myth that says women are treacherous; since women can't be trusted, clearly their ability to give life is the only thing worth having although the womb is tainted by their inferiority and sinful nature. And so we find that in order to affirm women's humanity, we need to re-think how we see women as mothers in our collective psyche, and it begins with re-examining the stories we tell about our primordial mothers. Here's an alternative story about Pandora:

> Earth-Mother has given the mortals life. This puzzled them greatly. They would stare curiously at one another, then turn away to forage for food. Slowly they found that hunger has many forms. One morning the humans followed an unusually plump bear cub to a hillside covered with bushes that hung heavy with red berries. They began to feast at once, hardly aware of the tremors beginning beneath their feet. As the quaking increased, a chasm gaped at the crest of the hill. From it arose Pandora with her Earthen *pithos*. The mortals were paralyzed with fear but the Goddess drew her into Her aura. "I'm Pandora, Giver of All

Gifts.: She lifted the lid from the large jar. From it She took a pomegranate, which became an apple, which became a lemon, which became a pear. "I bring you flowering trees that bear fruit, gnarled trees hung with olives and, this, the grapevine and that will sustain you." She reached into the jar for a handful of seeds and sprinkled them over the hillside. "I bring you plants for hunger and illness, for weaving and dyeing. Hidden beneath My surface you will find minerals, ore, and clay of endless form. "She took from the jar two flat stones. "Attend with care My plainest gift: I bring you flint." Then Pandora turned the jar on its side, inundating the hillside with Her flowing grace. The mortals were bathed in the changing colors of Her aura. "I bring you wonder, curiosity, memory. I bring you wisdom. I bring you justice with mercy. I bring you caring and communal bonds. I bring you courage, strength, endurance. I bring you loving kindness for all beings. I bring you the seeds of peace."[lxii]

Instead of releasing all evil from the mythological jar (Greeks had jars, not boxes) Pandora released all goodness, and we see this goodness all around us: just as women give life, earth gives us life too. Pandora's biblical counterpart, Eve, has similarly been blamed for unleashing death, evil, and despair into the world although she was the giver of all life. But what was her crime? According to the Bible there was none; she was tricked into taking the fruit by the serpent as she was unaware of evil and thus innocent. [lxiii] And yet, theologians have considered Eve cursed by God and punished with subjection to the man, while the man escaped a similar punishment. Essentially our theologians have acted just like the Pharisees who dragged the woman caught in adultery to Jesus: they didn't bring the man to be stoned with her.[lxiv] But why would God curse the very human who has the ability to give life when the first commandment was to be fruitful and fill the earth? The answer lies in the way envy causes us to say things we wouldn't otherwise. When those who give life are considered evil and those who take life are considered good, violence becomes part of goodness and life part of evil; death becomes the dream and life the nightmare. It's the foundation of patriarchy, but in reality there is no curse on life; *death* is the curse. When men claim special privileges based on their greater physical strength and ability to take life, they place themselves outside of the will of God, for God's will is life, not death.

Motherhood could have potentially made women equal to men already in the Victorian era, if it wasn't for housework. Housework is considered "women's work" and it's not a compliment; the work is dull and repetitive. The way housework is tied to women is seen in how parenting done by fathers has become widely accepted in cultures where women are legal adults, but dad still gets away with not doing the laundry or dishes; dad's time is fun time, mom does the rest, and there is a reason for it. Just as patriarchy has perpetuated itself by lodging itself into our institutions and making men's leadership appear so natural that it is almost supernatural, "women's work" is considered natural because women are *raised* to become mothers who do all the housework as explained by Nancy Chodorow:

> Culture and personality theory has shown that early experiences common to members of a particular society contribute to the formation of typical personalities organized around and preoccupied with certain relational issues. To the extent that females and males experience different interpersonal environments as they grow up, feminine and masculine personality will develop differently and be preoccupied with different issues. The structure of the family and family practices create certain differential relational needs and capacities in men and women that contribute to the reproduction of women as mothers.[lxv]

The family is where children learn what it means to be men and women. Little girls are expected to identify with mom and little boys are expected to identify with dad, and through this identification the children are expected to become normal, well-adjusted grownups. And perhaps they become exactly that, but none of it explains why girls are supposed to become mothers who do all the housework. Chodorow continues:

> Another prevalent assumption is that girls naturally identify with their mother as they grow up, and that this makes them into mothers. How and why this identification happens are left vague and unanalyzed. But as cognitive psychologists have shown, children identify with a parent of a particular gender because they have already learned that this is how to be appropriately feminine or masculine. Identification is a product of conscious teaching about gender differences, that is, a learning phenomenon. Psychoanalytic clinical studies illustrate particularly vividly how parents teach children about what biological gender differences are supposed to mean, and what their biology is supposed to entail for their adult role. The identification they describe takes place in a socially constructed, heavily value-laden context. Identification and learning clearly goes on, and helps to make women into mothers, but these processes are not sufficient.[lxvi]

So, what causes women to become mothers who do all the housework? One reason is our theologians and their insistence it is God's will for women to have children and take care of their homes. Secular patriarchy says much the same thing as men in heavy-handed patriarchal societies are socialized into rejecting parenting and housework as "women's work."[lxvii] As men reject parenting, women's exclusive mothering and over-investment creates a general and widespread contempt of women in patriarchal societies.

> Too much of mother results from the relative absence of the father and nearly exclusive maternal care provided by a woman isolated in a nuclear household. It creates men's resentment and dread of women, and their search for nonthreatening, undemanding, dependent, even infantile women — women who are "simple, and thus safe and warm." Through these same processes men come to reject, devalue, and even ridicule women and things feminine.[lxviii]

All of this begs the question, if women's exclusive mothering creates contempt in men, and this contempt causes further gender segregation in an endless cycle, shouldn't we attempt to reduce the contempt by including men in the great work of parenting? According to Chodorow the answer is a resounding yes! What is more important than having mom home all by herself is constancy of care and having only a few select people taking care of the child in order to foster trust and bonding.[lxix] These select people can, and should, include men, as "there is substantial evidence that nonbiological mothers, children, and men can parent just as adequately as biological mothers and can feel just as nurturant."[lxx] The underlying assumption behind women's exclusive mothering is the mistaken belief all biological mothers become adequate parents. This is not the case as the foster care system knows all too well. And it's perfectly reasonable as parenting isn't biological, it's psychological.

> The biological argument for women's mothering is based on facts that derive, not from our biological knowledge, but from our definition of the natural situation as this grows out of our participation in certain social arrangements. … Mothering is most eminently a psychologically based role. It consists in psychological and personal experience of self in relationship to child or children.[lxxi]

In other words, biology isn't destiny; if it was, human evolution would be impossible.[lxxii]

Although both secular and religious patriarchy pushes women nearly exclusively towards mothering and housework (as it places them under the man's authority), the patristic church had other ideas about the necessity of marriage and motherhood in the fourth century. Ambrose, the bishop of Milan (and the baptizer of Augustine), was an adamant supporter of lifelong celibacy, though he admitted the idea went against nature; and yet, it was precisely *because* it was against nature that celibacy was considered to be of a heavenly origin.[lxxiii] Although he knew fully well the "pagans" had their virgins (e.g., the Vestal Virgins), instead of being impressed, Ambrose didn't approve of chastity that was only for a set term and not based on morals; such celibacy couldn't possibly be sacred. At the same the ideal of motherhood can be found behind the ideal of perpetual sacred celibacy:

> So the holy Church, ignorant of wedlock, but fertile in bearing, is in chastity a virgin, yet a mother in offspring. She, a virgin, bears us her children, not by a human father, but by the Spirit. She bears us not with pain, but with the rejoicings of the angels. She, a virgin, feeds us, not with the milk of the body, but with that of the Apostle, wherewith he fed the tender age of the people who were still children.□ For what bride has more children than holy Church, who is a virgin in her sacraments and a mother to her people, whose fertility even holy Scripture attests, saying, "For many more are the children of the desolate than of her that hath an husband"? She has not an husband, but she has a Bridegroom, inasmuch as she, whether as the Church amongst nations, or as the soul in individuals, without any loss of modesty, she weds the Word of God as her eternal Spouse,

free from all injury, full of reason.[lxxiv]

The fourth-century church believed the end was imminent and there was therefore no need to continue to populate an already populated earth. The Kingdom of God needed to be filled with people, and although the method was different, the desired outcome was the same. Thus the patristic church followed the example of the previous centuries and the advice of Apostle Paul who recommended celibacy as a remedy against too much earthly care. That married women carried a heavier burden in marriage was widely recognized, and perpetual celibacy was offered as an escape from the pain of childbirth and odious husbands.[lxxv]

The most important question for our purposes is why Ambrose considered virginity to be moral. He didn't really say. We do know marriage was mandatory in Rome during the age of Augustus. The unmarried were punished with fines and we know Paul's advice for the Christians to remain unmarried would have created all sorts of trouble for them for that very reason. [lxxvi] But it still doesn't explain *why* virginity was considered moral—unless it had something to do with the idea of equality the early church still upheld as sacred. Sin was considered the cause of all the troubles we experience as humans and by remaining single Christians could avoid perpetuating the inequalities created by traditional Roman marriage. Thus singleness became a moral issue from the perspective of equality.

We can of course wonder why the fourth-century church didn't reform their ideas about marriage as the Bible is rather clear about mutual submission, but it was perhaps too much to ask of the church that had already given in to Roman mores in more than one area. It was easier to continue to tell people to remain single than to try to get rid of the third-century belief God had cursed Eve and as a consequence subjected all married women to their husbands. As a stark contrast, Mary, the second Eve, was presented as an obedient virgin, and see what good she accomplished with her virginal purity! The church would continue to give the choice to remain celibate to both men and women until the Reformation and the introduction of mandatory marriage into theology. But even before Luther appeared on the scene, another event altered the way mandatory marriages would be advertised in the future Protestant churches.

In the thirteenth century Thomas Aquinas wrote his *Summa Theologica,* a synthesis of Aristotle's philosophy and medieval theology. In his rather large work, Thomas added Aristotle's logic to the creation account as he was unable to explain the reason for the woman's creation before the entrance of sin without it.

> Further, subjection and limitation were a result of sin, for to the woman was it said after sin (Genesis 3:16): "Thou shalt be under the man's power"; and Gregory says that, "Where there is no sin, there is no inequality." But woman is naturally of less strength and dignity than man; "for the agent is always more honorable than the patient," as Augustine says (Gen. ad lit. xii, 16).

Therefore woman should not have been made in
the first production of things before sin."[lxxvii]

Thomas answered his own question with the following
statement: "As regards the individual nature, woman is
defective and misbegotten [i.e. an impotent male], "but "as
regards human nature in general, woman is not misbegotten,
but is included in nature's intention as directed to the work of
generation." Thomas concluded the woman's subjection is
twofold: the woman is under the man's authority from
creation as she is a defective human and order can exist only if
people are governed by those who are wiser, but sin caused a
subjection which is "servile, by virtue of which a superior
makes use of a subject for his own benefit."[lxxviii] And so we
find that with a few strokes of his pen, Thomas struck down
the choice the church had given women from the fourth
century: celibacy and independence, or motherhood and
subjection. Three centuries later Luther would seal the deal by
sending all women back home to have children and obey their
husbands in the likeness of Aristotle two thousand years
before him.

Chapter 5

"It is not dissent that is harmful to feminism but consensus."

Naomi Wolf

Waves bring all kinds of hidden treasures from the ocean, but they bring also up the remnants of an already extinguished life. The waves of feminism have not only challenged the existing power imbalance caused by the man's authority, they have also exposed patriarchy's underbelly, the violence it tries to hide from our modern sensibilities. We don't like violence. Actually, let me re-phrase that one—we don't like to experience real violence. We enjoy viewing violence on a screen, but only because we know it's fake, much the same way people say they love "a good murder" when talking about murder mysteries. Some claim our modern dislike of violence is caused by women taking over the world and making people "soft." This claim is centered on the idea the world is a violent place. It is a central belief in patriarchy that has kept it going for centuries: if the world is an inherently violent place our leaders must be able to tackle said violence and women can't be trusted because of their emotional nature. And so we find the inevitability of violence is tied to the overall concept of leadership favored by patriarchy—the subjection of people through fear and violence.

The central role in this drama is played by the strict father who wields authority in the home and society at large and sheds blood when needed. Women's role is to obey and uphold the man's authority, to give birth to children, and care for the home, the crucible of patriarchal authority. Patriarchy considers this arrangement moral, mainly because women are believed to be more nurturing and risk therefore coddling children, creating weak individuals prone to immoral behavior. Strength is a moral virtue, but more specifically, strength is considered to be a masculine virtue.[lxxix] Nurturing is a feminine virtue, women's virtue *par excellence*, but only when strictly controlled by masculine strength.[lxxx]

The intricate web of forced relationships is the source of the power structures that re-create themselves by denying the humanity of the enslaved and by giving women some measure of power. But although patriarchy gives some women a taste of power, most women won't fight too hard against their own subjection when the alternative is violence in the hands of those who rule over them. Millions of women experience violence, coercion, and threats due to the belief the man should have all authority in the home. The cruel irony of the situation is seen in how we as a society wonder why domestic violence victims don't leave, while everything is done to prevent them from leaving. In the eyes of patriarchy, the woman's submission absolves the man from the consequences of his actions; if the woman willingly accepts the treatment, no wrong has been done. That the man must use a whip to create the willing submission is just a sign that the woman is rebellious and deserves to be whipped. In other words, both submission and the refusal to submit are excuses for cruelty. No wonder then that patriarchy isn't enamored with feminism and its insistence women and children should be allowed to live free from the fear of violence.

Violence isn't the only method in patriarchy's training manual to prevent rebellion. The most effective method to subject people is to convince them they *deserve* to be subjected as subjection is a mindset.[lxxxi] Our minds can, and are, trained to accept the demands of obedience. Left alone the mind will seek to live as free; it doesn't know how to exist otherwise. And because the mind wants to be free, the training must begin early, from infancy if at all possible. To succeed, the mental conditioning must be thorough as seen in this rather macabre description of how slaves were literally created from otherwise free humans in the antebellum South:

> The way to create the perfect slave, accustom him to rigid discipline, demand from him unconditional submission, impress upon him his innate inferiority, develop in him a paralyzing fear of white men, train him to adopt the master's code of good behavior and instill in him a sense of complete dependence.[lxxxii]

Inferiority is a key component in the patriarchal conditioning, as inferiority coupled with fear forces people to adopt good behavior as a protective mechanism; nothing irritates those in power more than a subject who talks back and fails to show proper respect. But although good behavior works for a while, no human being can live without ever disagreeing with another. Therefore complete dependence is what ultimately keeps people in their subjection; few people choose starvation willingly. Let's review the list:

Rigid Discipline
Unconditional Submission
Innate Inferiority
Paralyzing Fear
Good Behavior
Complete Dependence

What dismantles the patriarchal training are the following:

Cooperation
Freedom of Choice
Equality
Love
Authenticity
Independence

As the man's word became law in the home and society at large, women found themselves forced to hold their tongues, and naturally so as there is no patriarchal submission without silence: power is made known by words and words carry power, therefore the powerless cannot be allowed to speak in the presence of the powerful. This silence isn't so much about if women should speak, but *when* they are allowed to speak and *what* they are allowed to say when they *do* speak. The Homeric poems provide us a vivid picture of women's silence before men:

> The true female condition in Homer was this: total exclusion from political power and participation in public life; subordination to the head of the family and submission to his punishment, and finally, ideological segregation. Forbidden to think about anything but domestic matters, the woman cannot even talk about male matters.[lxxxiii]

Left alone women are allowed to speak as much as they like. But in the presence of men they are expected to be silent; if they must speak they better be polite, so polite their words begin to lose meaning. And there is a reason for it: women's words are meant to sooth and assuage, instead of challenging.[lxxxiv] Aristotle even went so far as to say[lxxxv] —

Silence is a woman's glory

But the woman's silence, however glorious in the eyes of the Greeks, didn't manage to preserve the Greek way of life although ostensibly powerful enough to do so. The Romans decimated their cities and carried the once proud Greek citizens to Rome as slaves, citing "order" as *their* reason; a turn of events that would have left Aristotle infuriated as he believed the Hellens were noble and therefore deserving of freedom.

> The same principle applies to nobility. Hellenes regard themselves as noble everywhere, and not only in their own country, but they deem the barbarians noble only when at home, thereby implying that there are two sorts of nobility and freedom, the one absolute, the other relative. The Helen of Theodectes says: 'Who would presume to call me servant whoam on both sides sprung from the stem of the Gods?' What does this mean but that they distinguish freedom and slavery, noble and humble birth, by the two principles of good and evil? They think that as men and animals beget men and animals, so from good men a good man springs. But this is what nature, though she may intend it, cannot always accomplish. We see then that there is some foundation for this difference of opinion, and that all are either slaves by nature of freemen by nature, and also that there is in some cases a marked distinction between the two classes, rendering it expedient and right for the one to be slaves and the others to be masters: the

> one practicing obedience, the others exercising the authority and lordship which nature intended them to have.[lxxxvi]

The idea some are born to rule was deeply embedded in Greek thinking as people who lived during antiquity believed "real" humans didn't do manual work.[lxxxvii] (We have reversed their position in our modern times as we now believe "real" people work; hence our insistence women *shouldn't* work because they lack the man's reason). But it wasn't as simple as it seemed. It is here we find Aristotle's biggest mistake: he equated the ability to reason with humanity — only the rational are human and therefore exempt from manual labor. And because only the rational were human, slaves were considered property, or living tools, as they were believed to lack a deliberative faculty all together.[lxxxviii] And yet, even Aristotle recognized not every slave lacked a rational faculty and he tried to resolve the problem by saying some freeborn men ought to have been slaves, and vice versa, effectually decimating his own argument in the absence of any rear proof slavery was natural.[lxxxix]

One of the most important clarifications that needs to be made is the fact patriarchy isn't only about men ruling over women. It's about *some* men ruling over everyone else (those deemed less human) and slavery is just as much part of the patriarchal world as female subjection. And although women are relentlessly trained to accept their lesser role in life, the role given to men is far more unyielding. Women can act like men (at least occasionally) and be praised for it (if everything goes well) but men can't act like women. A man who acts like a woman, or in ways society considers feminine will be mercilessly censured. We see a similar rigidness in our class societies: if a poor person manages to rise from poverty against all odds he is congratulated, but a wealthy person cannot become poor without feeling deep shame. This tells us maleness and wealth are seen as something intrinsically good, femaleness and poverty as something fundamentally shameful. And all of this relates to how we value human life in general and how we expect to be treated: if we believe poverty and womanhood is something shameful, we will expect to be treated poorly and we will rarely object. In addition, if we believe we exist for others, we won't object when we are being used as we don't have a sense of self that could feel used, and that in itself causes us to remain silent.

All girls must learn how to speak
All women must learn how to speak up

Speech is one of the most important indicators of who has power in any given situation. When the Grimke sisters spoke against slavery in the early 19th century they were charged with the grave crime of speaking before a "promiscuous assembly," that is, a mixed audience of both men and women. Lucy Stone was a firsthand witness to the response given by the church.

A few years later, in 1837, the Pastoral Letter against the Grimke sisters was read from the pulpit. Lucy said her "Indignation blazed" when the minister, relishing each word, read the censure of women "who so far forget themselves as to itinerate in the character of public lectures and teachers." She told her cousin, who was with her, that "if I ever had anything to say in public, I should say it, and all the more because of that Pastoral Letter."[xc]

I have re-printed the Pastoral Letter here because I believe it to be of great interest as it highlights the sheer absurdity of the opposition women faced in the nineteenth century when they spoke in public.

Brookfield, June 27, 1837
Brethren and Friends,

Having assembled to consult upon the interests of religion within this commonwealth, we would now, as Pastors and Teachers, in accordance with the custom of this Association, address you on some of the subjects which at the present time appear to us to have an important bearing upon the cause of Christ. The first topic upon which we would speak, has respect to the perplexed and agitating subjects which are now common amongst us.

All that we would say at present with regard to
these subjects, is this: They should not be
forced on any church as matters for debate, at
the hazard of alienation and division. Once it
would have seemed strange even to hint that
members of churches could wish to force a
subject for debate upon their Pastor and their
brethren of the same church. But we are
compelled to mourn over the loss, in a degree,
of that deference to the pastoral office, which
no minister would arrogate, but which is at
once a mark of christian urbanity, and a
uniform attendant of the full influence of
religion upon individual character. If there be a
tendency in zeal upon these subjects to violate
the principles and rules of christian
intercourse, to interfere with the proper
pastoral influence, and to make the church into
which we flee from a troubled world for peace,
a scene of "doubtful disputations," there must
be something wrong in that zeal or in the
principles which excite it. If any are
constrained to adopt those principles, and to
use that zeal, we would affectionately and
solemnly caution them not to disturb the
influence of those ministers who think that the
promotion of personal religion among their
people, and the establishment of Christians in
the faith and comfort of the Gospel, is the

proper object of their ministry. We would call your attention to the importance of maintaining that respect and deference to the Pastoral office which is enjoined in Scripture, and which is essential to the best influence of the ministry on you and your children. One way in which this respect has been in some cases violated, is in encouraging lecturers or preachers on certain topics of reform to present their subjects within the parochial limits of settled pastors without their consent. Your minister is ordained of God to be your teacher, and is commanded to feed that flock over which the Holy Ghost hath made him overseer. If there are certain topics upon which he does not preach with the frequency, or in the manner that would please you, it is a violation of sacred and important rights to encourage a stranger to present them. Deference and subordination are essential to the happiness of society, and peculiarly so in the relation of a people to their pastor. Let them despise or slight him, and he ceases to do them good, and they cease to respect those things of which he is at once the minister and the symbol. There is great solemnity in those words: "Obey them that have the rule over you and submit yourselves; for they watch for your souls as they that must give account." It is because we desire the highest influence of the ministry upon you and your children, that we now exhort you to reverence that office which the ascending Redeemer selected from all his gifts as the highest token of his love and care for his people. We invite your attention to the dangers which at present seem to threaten the female character with wide spread and permanent injury. The appropriate duties and influence of women, are clearly stated in the New Testament. Those duties and that influence are unobtrusive and private, but the sources of mighty power. When the mild, dependent, softening influence of woman upon the sternness of man's opinions is fully exercised, society feels the effects of it in a thousand forms. The power of woman is in her dependence, flowing from the consciousness of that weakness which God has given her for her protection and which keeps her in those departments of life that form the character of individuals and of the nation. There are social influences which females use in promoting piety and the great objects of christian benevolence, which we cannot too highly commend. We appreciate the unostentatious prayers and efforts of woman, in advancing the cause of religion at home and abroad:--in Sabbath schools, in leading religious inquirers to their pastor for instruction, and in all such associated effort as becomes the modesty of her sex; and earnestly hope that she may abound more and more in these labours of piety and love. But when she assumes the place and tone of a man as a public reformer, our care and protection of her seem unnecessary, we put ourselves in self defence against her, she yields the power which God has given her for protection, and her character becomes unnatural. If the vine, whose strength and beauty is to lean upon the trellis work and half conceal its clusters, thinks to assume the independence and the overshadowing nature of the elm, it will not only cease to bear fruit, but fall in shame and dishonour into the dust. We cannot, therefore, but regret the mistaken conduct of those who encourage females to bear an obtrusive and ostentatious part in measures of reform, and countenance any of that sex who so far forget themselves as to itinerate in the character of public lecturers and teachers. We especially deplore the intimate acquaintance and promiscuous conversation of females with regard to things "which ought not to be named;" by which that modesty and delicacy which is the charm of domestic life, and which constitute the true influence of women in society are consumed, and the way opened, as we apprehend, for degeneracy and ruin. We say these things, not to discourage proper influences against sin, but to secure such reformation as we believe is scriptural and will be permanent. We would set before you, as specially important in the present times, the cultivation of private christian character, and private efforts for the spiritual good of individuals. If every Christian will faithfully endeavor so to live and act, so to discipline his natural disposition, and to make such attainments in goodness as to receive a testimony like that which Enoch had before his translation, that he pleases God, true piety will be universal, and pure religion will prevent the incursions of doctrinal and practical errors. We should remember that while we strive to do good, it is of the first importance that we be good. The improvement of his individual christian character, should be the first and great object with every one. To exercise the feelings of which the Savior has set us an example, to be like Him in the spirit and temper of our minds, is the surest way to secure the approbation and love of God. Without this, our public efforts in the cause of God and man, however extensive and successful, will profit us nothing. If Christians will labor privately to form individual minds, especially those of the young, to virtue and religion, they will hasten the universal prevalence of religion by the most effectual means. We commend the Sabbath School, and the Bible Class to the members of our churches as opportunities of extensive and enduring influence. The regular, uniform discharge of the duties of our stations in the fear of God, the influence of faith, hope, and charity, upon the heart and conduct, a growing acquaintance with the Bible as a means of true and safe zeal, an increasing knowledge of the way of salvation by Christ, as a matter of personal experience and hope, should be the aim and end of every member of our churches. That we may be examples to you in these things, pray for us continually. And may grace, mercy, and peace be upon you and yours, and upon the whole Israel of God, Amen.

All of the above could have been said in one simple sentence: only pastors are allowed to speak in public about matters that are important, as such speech is tied to the importance of the pastor's role. This pride-filled attitude is also tied to the financial realm: one of the great *Aha!* moments in a woman's life comes when she realizes the man's authority in the home is based on him being the provider, but in the church all women are more than welcomed, or I should say, mandated to support the minister the way Jesus was supported by women during his earthly walkabout. In other words, a woman is not allowed to make money if it gives her independence, but she is mandated to give money if it supports her own oppression. The thinly veiled self-importance expressed in the Pastoral Letter may amaze the modern reader, but it didn't amaze Sarah Grimke, who didn't waste any time to respond.

Haverhill, 7th Mo. 1837.
DEAR FRIEND--

When I last addressed thee, I had not seen the Pastoral Letter of the General Association. It has since fallen into my hands, and I must digress from my intention of exhibiting the condition of women in different parts of the world, in order to make some remarks on this extraordinary document. I am persuaded that when the minds of men and women become emancipated from the thralldom of superstition and traditions of men, the sentiments contained in the Pastoral Letter will be recurred to with as much astonishment as the opinions of Cotton Mather and other distinguished men of his day, on the subject of witchcraft; nor will it be deemed less wonderful, that a body of divines should gravely assemble and endeavor to prove that woman has no right to 'open her mouth for the dumb,' than it now is that judges should have sat on the trials of witches, and solemnly condemned nineteen persons and one dog to death for witchcraft. But to the letter. It says, we invite your attention to the dangers which at present seem to threaten the FEMALE CHARACTER with wide-spread and permanent injury. I rejoice that they have called the attention of my sex to this subject, because I believe if woman investigates it, she will soon discover that danger is impending, though from a totally different source from which the Association apprehends,--danger from those who, having long held the reins of usurped authority, are unwilling to permit us to fill that sphere which God created us to move in, and who have entered into league to crush the immortal mind of woman. I rejoice, because I am persuaded that the rights of woman, like the rights of slaves, need only be examined to be understood and asserted, even by some of those who are now endeavoring to smother the irrepressible desire for mental and spiritual freedom which glows in the breast of many, who hardly dare to speak their sentiments. The appropriate duties and influence of women are clearly stated in the New Testament. Those duties are unobtrusive and private, but the sources of mighty power. When the mild, dependent, softening influence of woman upon the sternness of man's opinions is fully exercised, society feels the effects of it in a thousand ways. No one can desire more earnestly than I do, that woman may move exactly in the sphere which her Creator has assigned her; and I believe her having been displaced from that sphere has introduced confusion into the world. It is, therefore, of vast importance to herself and to all the rational creation, that she ascertain what are her duties and her privileges as a responsible and immortal being. The New Testament has been referred to, and I am willing to abide by its decisions, but must enter my protest against the false translation of some passages by the MEN who did that work, and against the perverted interpretation by the MEN who undertook to write commentaries thereon. I am inclined to think, when we are admitted to the honor of studying Greek and Hebrew, we shall produce some various readings of the Bible a little different from those we now have. The Lord Jesus defines the duties of his followers in his Sermon on the Mount. He lays down grand principles by which they should be governed, without any reference to sex or condition:- Ye are the light of the world. A city that is set on a hill cannot be hid. Neither do men light a candle and put it tinder a bushel, but on a candlestick, and it giveth light unto all that are in the house.

Let your light so shine before men, that they may see your good works, and glorify your Father which is in Heaven. I follow him through all his precepts, and find him giving the same directions to women as to men, never even referring to the distinction now so strenuously insisted upon between masculine and feminine virtues: this is one of the anti-christian traditions of men which are taught instead of the commandments of God. Men and women were CREATED EQUAL; they are both moral and accountable beings, and whatever is right for man to do, is right for woman. But the influence of woman, says the Association, is to be private and unobtrusive; her light is not to shine before man like that of her brethren; but she is passively to let the lords of the creation, as they call themselves, put the bushel over it, lest peradventure it, might appear that the world has been benefited by the rays of her candle. So that her quenched light, according to their judgment, will be of more use than if it were set on the candlestick. Her influence is the source of mighty power. This has ever been the flattering language of man since he laid aside the whip as a means to keep woman in subjection. He spares her body; but the war he has waged against her mind, her heart, and her soul, has been no less destructive to her as a moral being. How monstrous, how anti-christian, is the doctrine that woman is to be dependent on man! Where, in all the sacred Scriptures, is this taught? Alas! she has too well learned the lesson which MAN has labored to teach her. She has surrendered her dearest RIGHTS, and been satisfied with the privileges which man has assumed to grant her; she has been amused with the show of power, whilst man has absorbed all the reality into himself. He has adorned the creature whom God gave him as a companion, with baubles and gewgaws, turned her attention to personal attractions, offered incense to her vanity, and made her the instrument of his selfish gratification, a plaything to please his eye and amuse his hours of leisure. Rule by obedience and by submission sway, or in other words, study to be a hypocrite, pretend to submit, but gain your point, has been the code of household morality which woman has been taught. The poet has sung, in sickly strains, the loveliness of woman's dependence upon man, and now we find it reechoed by those who profess to teach the religion of the Bible. God says, Cease ye from man whose breath is in his nostrils, for wherein is he to be accounted of? Man says, depend upon me. God says, HE will teach us of his ways. Man says, believe it not, I am to be your teacher. This doctrine of dependence upon man is utterly at variance with the doctrine of the Bible. In that book I find nothing like the softness of woman, nor the sternness of man: both are equally commanded to bring forth the fruits of the Spirit, love, meekness, gentleness, etc. But we are told, the power of woman is in her dependence, flowing from a consciousness of that weakness which God has given her for her protection. If physical weakness is alluded to, I cheerfully concede the superiority; if brute force is what my brethren are claiming, I am willing to let them have all the honor they desire; but if they mean to intimate, that mental or moral weakness belongs to woman, more than to man, I utterly disclaim the charge. Our powers of mind have been crushed, as far as man could do it, our sense of morality has been impaired by his interpretation of our duties; but no where does God say that he made any distinction between us, as moral and intelligent beings. We appreciate, say the Association, the unostentatious prayers and efforts of woman in advancing the cause of religion at home and abroad, in leading religious inquirers TO THE PASTOR for instruction. Several points here demand attention. If public prayers and public efforts are necessarily ostentatious, then Anna the prophetess, (or preacher,) who departed not from the temple, but served God with fastings and prayers night and day, and spake [sic] of Christ to all them that looked for redemption in Israel, was ostentatious in her efforts. Then, the apostle Paul encourages women to be ostentatious in their efforts to spread the gospel, when he gives them directions how they should appear, when engaged in praying, or preaching in the public assemblies. Then, the whole association of Congressional ministers are ostentatious, in the efforts they are making in preaching and praying to convert souls. But woman may be permitted to lead religious inquires to the PASTORS for instruction. Now this assuming that all pastors are better qualified to give instruction than woman. This I utterly deny. I have suffering too keenly from the teaching of man, to lead any one to him for instruction. The Lord Jesus says,--Come unto me and learn of me. He points his followers to no man; and when woman is made the favored instrument of rousing a sinner to his lost and helpless condition, she has no right to substitute any teacher for Christ; all she has to do is, to turn the contrite inquire to the Lamb of God which taketh away the sins of the world. More souls have probably been lost by going down to Egypt for help, and by trusting in man in the early stages of religious experience, than by any other error. Instead of the petition being offered to

God,- Lead me in thy truth, and TEACH me, for thou art the God of my salvation, instead of relying on the precious promises What man is he that feareth the Lord? Him shall HE TEACH in the way that he shall choose I will instruct thee and TEACH thee in the way which thou shalt go I will guide thee with mine eye the young convert is directed to go to man, as if he were in the place of God, and his instructions essential to an advancement in the path of righteousness. That woman can have but a poor conception of the privilege of being taught of God, what he alone can teach, who would turn the religious inquirer aside from the fountain of living waters, where he might slake his thirst for spiritual instruction, to those broken cisterns which can hold no water, and therefore cannot satisfy the panting spirit. The business of men and women, who are ORDAINED of GOD to preach the unsearchable riches of Christ to a lost and perishing world, is to lead souls to Christ, and not to Pastors for instruction. The General Association say, that 'when woman assumes the place and tone of man as a public reformer, our care and protection of her seem unnecessary; we put ourselves in self-defense against her, and her character becomes unnatural.' Here again the unscriptural notion is held up, that there is a distinction between the duties of men and women as moral beings; that what is virtue in man, is vice in woman; and women who dare to obey the command of Jehovah, 'Cry aloud, spare not, lift up thy voice like a trumpet, and show my people their transgression,' are threatened with having the protection of the brethren withdrawn. If this is all they do, we shall not even know the time when our chastisement is inflicted; our trust is in the Lord Jehovah, and in him is everlasting strength. The motto of woman, when she is engaged in the great work of public reformation should be,--The Lord is my light and my salvation; whom shall I fear? The Lord is the strength of my life; of whom shall I be afraid?: She must feel, if she feels rightly, that she is fulfilling one of the important duties laid upon her as an accountable duties laid upon her as an accountable being, and that her character, instead of being unnatural, is in exact accordance with the will of Him to whom, and to no other, she is responsible for the talents and the gifts confided to her. As to the pretty simile, introduced into the Pastoral Letter, If the vine whose strength and beauty is to lean upon the trellis work, and half conceal its clusters, thinks to assume the independence and the overshadowing nature of the elm, etc. I shall only remark that it might well suit the poet's fancy, who sings of sparkling eyes and coral lips, and knights in armor clad; but it seems to me utterly inconsistent with the dignity of a Christian body, to endeavor to draw such an anti-scriptural distinction between men and women. Ah! How many of my sex feel in the dominion, thus unrighteously exercised over them, under the gentle appellation of protection, that what they have leaned upon has proved a broken reed at best, and oft a spear.

Thine in the bonds of womanhood,
SARAH M. GRIMKE

Pastoral letter = 0 points   Sarah Grimke = 10 points

Because of the prevailing negative attitudes against women's public speech during the nineteenth-century, one of the first orders of business for the first wave feminists was to gain the right for women to speak in public. It was easier said than done. At the 1840 World Anti-Slavery Convention in London, Lucretia Mott and Elizabeth Cady Stanton found themselves restricted to the gallery instead of being allowed on the main floor, because the presence of women was said to lower the dignity of the convention due to Genesis 3:16.[xci] This begs naturally the question, what exactly is meant by dignity and what are we saying when we claim women aren't allowed to speak in conventions, because it would lower the dignity of that said convention? If this dignity is a quality in a person who is therefore worthy of honor and respect, are we not saying there is something fundamentally wrong with women; that they do not possess the kind of quality in themselves that would make them worthy of honor and respect? And this question leads the most damning of all questions: what if men evoke the concept of dignity to secure their own privilege in order to avoid having to show proper respect toward women?

As a response to the blatant discrimination they had experienced at the Anti-Slavery Convention, Lucretia Mott and Elizabeth Stanton organized the Seneca Falls Convention in 1848 in New York with the explicit intent of addressing women's rights, or rather, the lack of rights. Sixty-eight women and thirty-two men signed the Declaration of Sentiments, a document that mimicked the Declaration of Independence, and that sought to give equal rights to women. The convention was a huge success, and as to be expected, heavily criticized and ridiculed. *Oneida Whig* published an article that asked, "Was there ever such a dreadful revolt?" And the *Mechanic's Advocate* didn't mince their words:

> We are sorry to see that the women in several parts of this State are holding what they call "Woman's Rights Conventions," and setting forth a formidable list of those rights in a parody upon the Declaration of American Independence....

The women who attend these meetings, no doubt at the expense of their more appropriate duties, act as committees, write resolutions and addresses, hold much correspondence, make speeches, &c., &c. They affirm, as among their rights, that of unrestricted franchise, and assert that it is wrong to deprive them of the privilege to become legislators, lawyers, doctors, divines, &c., &c.; and they are holding Conventions and making an agitatory movement, with the object in view of revolutionizing public opinion and the laws of the land, and changing their relative position in society in such a way as to divide with the male sex the labors and irresponsibilities of active life in every branch of art, science, trades, and professions.... Now, it requires no argument to prove that this is all wrong. Every true hearted female will instantly feel that this is unwomanly, and that to be practically carried out, the males must change their position in society to the same extent in an opposite direction, in order to enable them to discharge an equal share of the domestic duties which now appertain to females, and which must be neglected, to a great extent, if women are allowed to exercise all the "rights" that are claimed by these Convention-holders.

Although the ridicule was widespread, there were also

positive responses. One was published by Henry Montgomery, the editor of *Daily Advertiser* (Rochester, NY).

> The harmony of this great movement in the cause of freedom would not be perfect, if women were still to be confined to petticoats, and men to breeches. There must be an "interchange" of these "commodities" to complete the system. Why should it not be so? Can women not fill an office, or cast a vote, or conduct a campaign, as judiciously and vigorously as men? And, on the other hand, can not men "nurse" the babies, or preside at the wash-tub, or boil a pot as safely and as well as women? If they can not, the evil is in that arbitrary organization of society which has excluded them from the practice of these pursuits. It is time these false notions and practices were changed, or, rather, removed, and for the political millennium foreshadowed by this petticoat movement to be ushered in. Let the women keep the ball moving, so bravely started by those who have become tired of the restraints imposed upon them by the antediluvian notions of a Paul or the tyranny of man.[xcii]

Even today we see the same mixed reactions toward feminism. The intrepid first wave feminists are portrayed as gentle and genteel in an effort to discredit the work of modern women. Although portrayed as gentle and maternal by modern patriarchy, Elizabeth Stanton didn't fear other people's opinions, nor did she let anyone stop her from speaking in public. Susan B. Anthony, Stanton's best friend, was also popular lecturer — *and* a believer in civil disobedience. In 1872 Anthony cast her ballot in the presidential elections. Two weeks later she was arrested, and eventually fined $100. She never paid the fine. Also Lucy Stone defied cultural norms when she insisted on attending college, although her father's response, "Is the child crazy?" was less than encouraging. Stone became the first woman to graduate from college in Massachusetts and a popular lecturer as all other professional avenues were closed to women in the nineteenth century. It was in fact in Oberlin College that Stone met her future sister-in-law, Antoinette Brown, the first woman to be ordained as minister in 1853. Having married Henry Brow Blackwell, Stone caused a scandal when she refused to be known by her married name. None of these women were exactly the mild and gentle "little women" we're expected to believe they were. Mary, Mother of Jesus, has been given the same treatment. The teen who defied her whole society and had a child out of wedlock is portrayed as silent, obedient, and gentle. All of this is done deliberately to strip women from their own agency in order to assign their successes to men who are seen as giving these rights willingly, or at least as soon as the subject was brought to their attention, even if it had to be done every year over the course of seven decades.

Simone de Beauvoir wrote famously about the woman being the "other" the man cannot quite understand or accept. Instead of being who they are naturally, all women have to *become* women.

> It is hard to know any longer if women still exist, if they will always exist, if there should women at all, what place they hold in this world, what place they should hold. "Where are the women?" asked a short-lived magazine recently. But first, what is a woman? "Tota mulier in utero: she is a womb," some say. Yet speaking of certain women, the experts proclaim, "They are not women," even though they have a uterus like the others. Everyone agrees that there are females in the human species; today, as in the past, they make up about half of humanity; and yet we are told that "femininity is in jeopardy"; we are urged, "Be women, stay women, become women." So not every female human being is necessarily a woman; she must take part in this mysterious and endangered reality known as femininity.[xciii]

So what is a woman? Patriarchy has a simple answer: a woman is a human being who is properly feminine. But this begs the question, what does it mean to be properly feminine? No one agrees, yet, every generation has had something to say about it. Here, surprisingly, Aristotle gives us something to consider about the "otherness" of women:

> Some things are said to be the same in this sense, other are the same but their own nature, in as many senses as that which is one by its own nature is so; for both the things whose matter is one either in kind or in number, and those whose essence is one, are said to be the same. Clearly, therefore, sameness is a unity of the being either of more than one thing or of one thing when it is treated as more than one. i.e. when we say a thing is the same as itself; for we treat it as two. Things are called 'other' if either their kinds or their matters of the definitions of their essence are more than one; and in general 'other' has meanings opposite to those of the 'the same.' ... The term 'other in species' is applied to things which being of the same genus are not subordinate the one to the other, or which being in the same genus have a difference, or which have a contrariety in their substance; and contraries are other than one another in species (either all contraries are those things whose definitions differ in the infima species of the genus (e.g. man and horse are indivisible in genus but their definitions are different), and

those which being in the same substance have a difference. 'The same in species' has the various meanings opposite to these.[xciv]

From a male point of view the woman is the "other sex" for she is a female human compared to the male human, but contrary to patriarchy's view, this "other" isn't subordinate. In other words, if men see women as "other," the only thing they see is women's humanity in relation to their own humanity. Women may *become* women, but they are born human.

Another related question is, "What do women want?" Just as with the question, "What is a woman?" also this question is made moot by the systematic denial of choices available for women—the regular complaint made by all waves of feminism. How is a woman supposed to want anything when all the decisions are already made for her, when her life is already mapped out for her, a life that consists of silence and obedience? And it is not a new complaint. Already several thousand years ago, men gave other men advice how to subject and silence women:

> It was around 2000 B.C. that an Egyptian writer, Ptah Hotep, put patriarchal beliefs as clearly as anyone in the early civilizations: "If you are a man of note, found for yourself a household, and love your wife at home, as it beseems. Fill her belly, clothe her back. . . . But hold her back from getting the mastery. Remember that her eye is her stormwind, and her vulva and mouth are her

strength."[xcv]

Not much has changed in four thousand years. *The Taming of the Shrew* was William Shakespeare's contribution to the question how to create the perfect wife. Petruchio marries the ill-mannered and hot-tempered Katherine and transforms her into a perfectly obedient wife through the regular patriarchal training methods. As a result of this "taming," Katherine proceeds to lecture other women about wifely obedience:

> Thus in plain terms: your father hath consented
> That you shall be my wife, your dowry 'greed on,
> And will you, nill you, I will marry you.
> Now Kate, I am a husband for your turn,
> For by this light, whereby I see thy beauty—
> Thy beauty that doth make me like thee well—
> Thou must be married to no man but me,
> For I am he am born to tame you, Kate,
> And bring you from a wild Kate to a Kate
> Conformable as other household Kates.
> Here comes your father. Never make denial.
> I must and will have Katherine to my wife.
> …
> Thy husband is thy lord, thy life, thy keeper,
> Thy head, thy sovereign, one that cares for thee,
> And for thy maintenance commits his body
> To painful labour both by sea and land,
> To watch the night in storms, the day in cold,
> Whilst thou liest warm at home, secure and safe,

And craves no other tribute at thy hands
But love, fair looks, and true obedience,
Too little payment for so great a debt.

. . .

My mind hath been as big as one of yours,
My heart as great, my reason haply more,
To bandy word for word and frown for frown;
But now I see our lances are but straws,
Our strength as weak, our weakness past compare,
That seeming to be most which we indeed least are.
Then vail your stomachs, for it is no boot,
And place your hands below your husband's foot,
In token of which duty, if he please,
My hand is ready, may it do him ease.[xcvi]

Because patriarchy is all about control, wildness must be eradicated; wild animals and nature in general scares the patriarchal mind. Violence is acceptable, but only as a means to control, not to devour. Accordingly, the patriarchal myth whispers to the man the woman is someone who is ready to devour him as seen in a quote by Ambrose Bierce, "Woman would be more charming if one could fall into her arms without falling into her hands."[xcvii] It is of course an absurd fear as women are human and humans know right from wrong. And yet, several thousand years of patriarchal insistence women aren't as human as men has created an irrational fear that is hard to eradicate.

Wildness isn't a problem only in women; it's a similar problem in men as patriarchy needs marriage to keep itself going, which means both men and women have to get on with the program. If sex is readily available, there is less incentive for people to marry, and so our modern patriarchal societies insist women need to "tame" men by crossing their legs and expecting a ring before undressing. This logic follows Sigmund Freud's conclusion our primordial instincts consist of *Eros* (sex) and *Thanatos* (death): women need to tame the man's instinct to have sex with every woman, and men need to tame the woman's instinct to murder every man. There's just one problem with this thought: the old Roman's believed women were sexually insatiable and that every man had a right to kill with impunity at the battlefield, the arena, and their own homes. This begs the question, does anyone really need to be tamed? If we *do* need to tame people, how is it supposed to be done and by who? If no one needs to be tamed, perhaps some measure of wildness is not only to be expected, but also desirable?

If we shouldn't be docile to the point of oblivion, why do we find women lecturing other women about wifely obedience? The answer is rather simple: women believe they will gain power through obedience. It may seem rather counterintuitive, but in a world ruled by a complex hierarchy where the top is beyond most people's reach, people accept less if it means they will gain more than their neighbors; even the smallest chicken wants to rank high in the pecking order. And so we find women working against their own interests as long as they keep on getting something out of it. And as long as they do, men will keep on occupying the centers of existence.

Chapter 6

"People follow only authority."

Sigmund Freud

Children love being at the center of attention. Try watching a movie or a sports game with a toddler in the room and the toddler will invariably block the view. Most of us learn to share our common spaces as we get older, but some will continue to place themselves in the center, expecting to remain there. It is especially true of people who believe they belong at the centers of power and who aren't willing to share that space with others. Our human institutions—family, religion, education, economics, and politics—form these centers of power. As already noted, patriarchy has managed to reproduce itself largely because it found a way to make itself part of our common human institutions. As a result, all five institutions have been the man's sphere of action and women have been soundly excluded from all of them as described by Elizabeth Janeway:

> "Normal people," in short, are normal men. What happens in man's world is the stuff we go by judging the past, coping with the present, and

planning for the future. Century after century of experience in running the world has persuaded men not that they know a way to do it, but that the way they do it is right. In times of social strain they may begin to wonder about their achievements and suspect that something may have gone wrong, but they continue to believe that they will solve the problems which have cropped up, solve them alone and by old methods, because they are the members of the human race who know how to do this. Even in bad times women are seldom welcome in man's world. On occasion they have been seen as scapegoats, responsible for the decline and fall of the normal male command of the situation, and firmly exiled from the arena of action.[xcviii]

Feminism's success in de-mythologizing the center opened it up to women, but although women can now be technically included, it doesn't mean they always are. One of the longest standing arguments in favor of the exclusion of women from leadership is the assumed incompetence of women and the even more widely assumed lack of common sense and justice.[xcix] Delilah and Jezebel stand as biblical examples of this kind of thinking. Had Delilah not caused Samson to lose his strength by betraying his secret all would have been well, and had Jezebel not been quite so evil things would have turned out differently for Israel. While everyone's eyes are focused on the women, everyone forgets conveniently all the men who worshiped idols, raped, pillaged and plundered, killed prophets, and brought God's wrath on the land in the form of Assyrian and Babylonian armies. But that is business as usual we are told: if we're going to experience disaster, we'll rather experience it having men as our leaders. And however strange that argument may sound there is a logical reason behind it: it has to do with this continuously re-emerging idea women are emotional, men are rational. Although men are just as likely to bring us to the brink of disaster, we are more willing to let them try in the first place just because we believe them to be more rational and therefore more capable. Women can try, and if they succeed they are considered to be men rather than women. If they fail, they have provided further proof women shouldn't be trusted to lead in the first place. This double standard has effectively banned women from pursuing leadership, and continues to do so although more and more women are braving the hostile environment.

Not all institutions exclude women in the same way at the same time, because not all institutions have the same amount of power and influence at any given time. The state has had to bow down to religion in one century, only to call it the opium of the masses in the next. The family has been considered, if not immoral, then at least worth less than the celibate life, whereas another era has worshiped the family as the source of all human happiness. As institutions have battled for power, women have found their opportunities rising and falling with every change.

Religious patriarchy had an ironclad argument to keep women away from all centers of power in "God say —." Once it was gone, the argument for women's exclusion was weakened. The secularization of society allowed politics, finance, and education to begin to accept the participation of women in leadership, causing religion to begin to try to reverse the trend by making politics, finance, and education its personal business. The proliferation of religious organizations such as *Focus on the Family* and the inroads of these organizations into the forbidden territories of politics testify of this discontent. The results have been more or less enlightening. As religion has struggled to uphold itself as the great arbitrator of morals, it has also made a point in naming feminism the great culprit of declining morality. The tendency to scapegoat and silence those who are far from the center is a recognized tactic to prevent people from being taken seriously. This was also recognized by bell hooks:

> Within institution shaped by white supremacist capitalist patriarchal biases, there is little hope that individuals who are interested in developing psychological theories and practices that address the dilemmas facing African American will find support. When this reality is linked to a culture of shame within diverse black

communities that silences attempts by black folks to name our woundedness, a climate of repression and suppression prevails.[c]

What makes our institutions particularly oppressive is the insistence some should talk while others listen. It begins at home, where children are expected to be "seen but not heard"; it continues in the school where students listen silently; it bleeds into religion where laity listens silently to the preacher; in finances money talks, and in the political realm the voters listen to political speeches without getting a change to voice their opinions other than through the silent ballot. Everywhere we look some are silenced while others talk and make decisions for everyone else without their input. As already noted, words have power and power gives privileges. It's the reason patriarchy insists only those who have power have the right to speak, because speech is a privilege given to the powerful in the patriarchal world.

Because speech is a privilege in the patriarchal world, some women think feminism, and its insistence women should be allowed to speak freely, is something they can use to get ahead of others. But feminism that is about personal privilege is about as useful as a decade old guidebook; it says all the right things but the information leads the traveler to all the wrong places. When we use feminism to give ourselves more power we defeat the purpose of feminism: it is supposed to empower *all* women, not just some at the expense of others. Speech may be considered a privilege by patriarchy, but it shouldn't be, for being a human being is not a privilege that can be granted or denied, it's a metaphysical reality.

Humans *are*, just like God *is*

And this thought leads us to consider the simple fact that since patriarchy hides behind our institutions, and since our institutions decide what is and what isn't a privilege, all privilege reveals its patriarchal origin. In the political realm, for example, legal rights can be, and have been, granted or denied because they have been considered privileges. Women's right to vote, for example, was denied because voting was considered to be a privilege:

> "Suffrage is not a right. It is a privilege that may
> or may not be granted. Politics is no place for a
> women [sic] consequently the privilege should
> not be granted to her."[ci]

Sometimes, and often unintentionally, the personal gets mixed up with the political. Abortion and contraceptives are discussed on the political arena *precisely* because they are considered privileges instead of decisions made with the help of medical professionals (we don't hear politicians talk about whether people should take aspirins or not). The discussion was moved to the political realm because patriarchy used laws to make abortion and contraceptives illegal and women had to the take the battle to the courts. Because the matter was settled in courts it was no longer seen as a personal decision; it had become a public decision and therefore discussed in public. And because it is discussed in public, everyone now believes they are entitled to an opinion about the morality of a private decision that is none of their business.

The tantalizing center is the secret of every privilege, and although we all enjoy some measure of privilege at some point of our lives, privilege that hides behind our institutions isn't always clearly seen, and that makes it difficult to expose and even more difficult to eradicate, especially since people who speak about authority and the necessity of obedience are always at the center or very close to it. A woman can happily speak about the husband's authority because just talking about it gives her a sense of power; she is doing (in patriarchy's opinion) the right thing and it's an empowering feeling. People who reject authority do so usually because they are far from the center, and most of these people are women.

The conversations about who belongs in the center can become awkward when the marginalized want to join in, especially when the challenge comes from women. The patriarchal default expects men to hog the limelight and women to accept it with a cheerful smile—a woman who doesn't accept her "role" is called a man-hating Jezebel or a bitter old maid who doesn't know how to attract a man. In other words, not only should women be quiet, they are also told not to compete with men for space. Co-operation is needed to make things happen, but when it comes to women, co-operation usually means taking the back seat. Men are expected to compete; women are expected to smile and cheer them on. And this has to do with the fact women are said to belong to the personal domestic sphere while men belong to the public sphere. As we noted above, when the personal is brought to the public, it becomes everyone's business. No wonder second wave feminists insisted on the following slogan:

"Personal is political"

The above slogan was made famous in the late 1960s to make women visible in the political arena and to highlight the abuses that were happening in the patriarchal home. It was an important and necessary step towards freeing women from the man's authority in the home, but the slogan missed an important point: *nothing will change as long as we fail to see the patriarchal home has always mirrored the power structures of the patriarchal state.* The political is already personal as women's subjection in the home begins with the laws formed and sanctified by the state.

The patriarchal state has a long and illustrious past. Already Plato divided the state into guardians, defenders, and artisans, and the individual human into reason, will, and appetite, which led him to argue that just as the guardians rule over the artisans with the help of the defenders, reason should rule over the appetite through the will within an individual person. Augustine took this thought to its logical conclusion when he argued the man should rule over the woman as reason rules over the appetite in the home, echoing the power structure of the patriarchal state, as he believed the woman causes the man to sin in the same way as passions causes us to become unjust.[cii] And it is here we find the source of the problem of personal being political: if the state should regulate our personal lives, we have no valid reason to reject the man's authority in the home unless we do something about the patriarchal ideology hidden in our institutions. Although the patriarchal state and its spokespersons talk about equality, especially when confronted with the worst of its own evils, it was the state—as embodied by the Greek *polis*—that segregated men and women into separate spheres and gave men authority over women, which means the state isn't going to desegregate men and women unless the state is first stripped off its patriarchal bias. And that can only be done when all citizens are equally represented in the centers of power. A government of men benefits only those who are men. We need women in our government if we want the state to regulate the home without giving men any more power than they already have. This truth is vividly seen in the changes that took place in Roman marriage in the second century CE.

If the life of the cities was to continue, the

discipline and the solidarity of the local elites and their ability to control their own dependents had to be mobilized with greater self-consciousness than ever before. A sense of public discipline had to reach deeper into the private lives of the notables as the price for maintaining the status quo of the second century A.D. In the Late Republic and early Empire the womenfolk of public men had been treated as peripheral beings, who contributed little or nothing to the public character of their husbands. They were considered "little creatures," whose behavior and relations to their husbands were of no real concern to the all-male world of politicians. They might sap the characters of their males by sensuality; they might even inspire them to heroic improvidence through genuine love; they frequently emerged as strong resources of courage and good counsel in difficult times. But the married relationship in itself carried little weight on the public stage. Much of what we call the "emancipation of women" in upper-class Roman circles in the Early Empire had been a freedom born of contempt. The little creatures could do what they liked, as long as it did not interfere with the serious play of male politics. Divorce was quick and simple; adultery, though it might unleash occasional savage revenge on wife and lover, in no way affected the husband's public standing. In the age of the Antonines the sense of the relative neutrality of upper-class marriage arrangements collapsed. The *concordia*, the *homonia*, of the good marriage was now brought forward (often as a conscious revival of the imagined discipline of the archaic Roman past) to act as a resonant new symbol of all other forms of social harmony.[ciii]

When the patriarchal state regulates the patriarchal home we don't get more rights and freedoms for women. Instead we get more control, and that control is always given to the man.

The patriarchal system gives all the power to the man at the precise moment when he shouldn't have any, and takes away all protection from the woman when she needs it the most. The same is seen in slavery: masters have the power to force slaves to obey, but slaves don't have the power to force their masters to treat them well. Contrary to the deliberate patriarchal power imbalance, the Bible requires the most humility from us when we want to give the least amount of love and consideration to others. This is succinctly described by the brief letter Paul sent to Philemon concerning his runaway slave, Onessimus. Paul expected Philemon to treat Onessimus as a brother — not a slave — and show him the same kind of consideration he would have wanted to receive himself if the positions were reversed. Although patriarchy gives more power to certain people to enable them to get what they want, God gives people power to enable them to dismantle existing power imbalances. The goal isn't power for power's sake, but power for the sake of ending injustice wherever it is found. This is one of the main reasons why patriarchy and the Bible are at odds with each other.

The above of course begs the question, why do we have such a thing as *religious patriarchy* that uses the Bible to defend its views? Although a contradiction in terms, the existence of religious patriarchy can be easily explained: when faced with opposition, if patriarchy isn't able to destroy its opponent, it brings it close and disarms it. We see this clearly in history books. Having failed to wipe out Christianity through persecution, patriarchal Rome made it the state religion in the fourth century. It didn't take long for the Gospel to change from a bold proclamation of freedom to one of subserviency as people were told to obey those in power. If they obeyed well, their lot in heaven would be one of perpetual bliss; if they didn't, their lot would be one of perpetual damnation. Heaven, hell, and hierarchy became symbols of the new power religious patriarchy wielded to either reward or punish, and slaves and women were the first ones to feel the consequences of this new power structure.

Since heaven and hell are tied to morals and our morality is decided by those who rule, failure to live a moral life according to the dictates of the powerful came with dire warnings of a future punishment. Here's an example:

And are we to suppose that the soul, which is invisible, in passing to the true Hades, which like her is invisible, and pure, and noble, and on her way to the good and wise God, whither, if God will, my soul is also soon to go-that the soul, I repeat, if this be her nature and origin, is blown away and perishes immediately on quitting the body as the many say? That can never be, dear Simmias and Cebes. The truth rather is that the soul which is pure at departing draws after her no bodily taint, having never voluntarily had connection with the body, which she is ever avoiding, herself gathered into herself (for such abstraction has been the study of her life). And what does this mean but that she has been a true disciple of philosophy and has practiced how to die easily? And is not philosophy the practice of death? … But the soul which has been polluted, and is impure at the time of her departure, and is the companion and servant of the body always, and is in love with and fascinated by the body and by the desires and pleasures of the body, until she is led to believe that the truth only exists in a bodily form, which a man may touch and see and taste and use for the purposes of his lusts-the soul, I mean, accustomed to hate and fear and avoid the intellectual principle, which to the bodily eye is dark and invisible, and can be attained only by

> philosophy-do you suppose that such a soul as this will depart pure and unalloyed? ... and these must be the souls, not of the good, but of the evil, who are compelled to wander about such places in payment of the penalty of their former evil way of life; and they continue to wander until the desire which haunts them is satisfied and they are imprisoned in another body.

Sounds like something someone pulled out of an old theology book, doesn't it? But in reality, it is an excerpt from *Phaedo*, written by Plato.[civ] The conviction we are going to be punished after death for having failed to live a moral life here on earth can be a great impetus for conformity, and the Greeks knew this as just as well as the Christians who borrowed the idea of Hades from the Greeks. But this begs the question, if our two choices are obedience to oppressive institutions or eternal death, isn't it a little bit like asking the mouse to avoid the mousetrap by placing the cheese on it and having the cat guard the rest of the kitchen? Since the belief in eternal torment is so deeply connected to forced subjection, feminism has traditionally questioned the existence of hell. Antoinette Brown Blackwell, for example, began to question eternal torment while pastoring her first church.

> The assumption of an angry, vengeful God who condemned people to eternal damnation in the absence of a particular pattern of salvation

became an untenable doctrine for Brown
Blackwell, to believe, and even more, to proclaim
to her congregation.[cv]

Blackwell had a point: why would God still be angry after
God had already ended the enmity, especially since God wills
all to be saved?[cvi] The same could also be framed a little
differently: why do our institutions get to decide whom God
condemns by creating a morality that benefits the institution
itself? There is nothing particularly moral about such an
arrangement, and it has always been feminism's greatest
complaint against the prevailing status quo. If we must live
moral lives, what precisely *is* moral about the way our
institutions create our morality?

Since patriarchy is the invisible hand that moves all things
behind the scenes, attempts to share the existing power in a
more equitable manner is seen as something unnatural, a fight
against nature. The reason behind all of it is the silent
conductor of the entire orchestra — money. It's not only
feminism that has been considered immoral in this battle for
rights; every attempt to end classism has been met with the
same kind of resistance, as described by Gustavo Gutierrez:

> Structural analysis has thus played an important
> part in building up the picture of the world to

which liberation theology addresses itself. The use of this analysis has had its price, for although the privileged of this world can accept the existence of human poverty on a massive scale and not be overawed by it (after all, it is something that cannot be hidden away in our time), problems begin when the causes of this poverty are pointed to them. Once causes are determined, then there is talk of "social injustice," and the privileged begin to resist. This is especially true when to structural analysis there is added a concrete historical perspective in which personal responsibilities come to light. But it is the conscientization and resultant organization of poor sectors that rouse the greatest fears and the strongest resistance.[cvii]

Poverty is a mandatory part of the patriarchal world, for if those who rule are to have more, others must have less. It is impossible to climb the steep steps of the patriarchal class hierarchy without the help of society and that is exactly what the patriarchal system is designed to prevent. At the same time, when we talk about the patriarchal hierarchy there is a general assumption all women find themselves at the bottom. This is however far from the truth. The patriarchal hierarchy is like a great elevator that anyone can ride to get to the top—if they can get on it, that is. And a lot of women do. When rights are considered a privilege and a men-versus-women battle instead of being part of a much larger conversation, we tend to lose sight of the overall effects of patriarchy and that blinds us to our own tendency to oppress others to gain more for ourselves. It makes no sense from the perspective of creating happy, thriving human communities, but few think of community when they are busy amassing wealth for themselves. It is in their advantage that poverty forces people to work for less than they need to live; cheap labor means more wealth for the already wealthy in a perpetual cycle of injustice.

Money is essential for us humans since we have decided that we need money to make trades equitable. No one would trade a house for a shoe; hence our need for a medium that creates a fair trade. Money isn't the problem; it is rather the amount we expect to spend on ourselves that is the problem. Plato was of the opinion all of the passions (e.g., food, sex, pleasure) could be summed up under the general term "money-loving." As a result he was adamantly against the passions as he believed they caused people to become unjust. It is true that if we aren't careful we begin to believe we exist to accumulate things instead of using things to live well. Our tendency to love things instead of people explains why we approve of the patriarchal hierarchy so very easily as not only do we have a tendency to accept that which we are already familiar with, we are also more likely to accept an ideology that gives us more than it costs us, especially since life can be a struggle; few have been willing to give up the excess that could potentially save the day tomorrow.

Since the wrongness of wealth comes from the means of acquiring the wealth, not the amount itself, the question how we should acquire money brings us to equity versus equality. Patriarchy insists equity is the only reasonable way for us to gain wealth, but it hides behind itself the deprivation of opportunities; the rags to riches stories are one in a million. Equality, on the other hand, dictates everyone must get equal opportunities and our abilities decide the outcome. Equality and equity are naturally about more than just how to make money in an ethical manner; it is also about how our institutions create and perpetuate injustice in the guise of morality. It is here the patriarchal dislike of equality shows why equity is favored as the only solution: our inability to know what kind of advantages people should be given to create an even playing field creates injustice especially when those who rule our societies, already awash in biases and favoritism, makes those choices. Equity will always favor a group, or groups, over others giving only a few the opportunities they need to realize their potential. And it is exactly how patriarchy likes it.

Equality insists everyone must be given equal opportunities from childhood on as rights are given on the basis of our humanity. This means also women must be given equal opportunities and it is precisely what patriarchy refuses to do. As a result, women who want to participate in leadership in any of the centers of power are told their presence is immoral, simply because the men who are already there don't want them there. Hence, to make women's presence in institutional leadership a familiar and natural part of life we need to add more women. But that's the whole problem as patriarchy insists women just aren't smart enough to lead.

Chapter 7

"Most women have no characters at all."

Alexander Pope

The human mind is a mystery we can only begin to hope to understand, and yet, we must understand its workings if we are going to live as fully as possible. What made ancient philosophy largely theoretical and therefore unhelpful was its insistence the mind consists of reason, will, and passions, and that human behavior is predictable because it is guided by reason. Sigmund Freud rejected the ancient conclusion as he found another element at work—the unconscious. The unconscious is a part of ourselves we cannot consciously access, but that nevertheless affects us. Yet, although Freud believed in the power of the unconscious, even he was reluctant to go any further than the Oedipus complex to find what the unconscious was hiding according to his former analysand Carl Jung:

> These fears are found not only among persons who are frightened by the picture Freud painted of the unconscious; they also troubled the originator of psychoanalysis himself, who confessed to me that it was necessary to make a

dogma of his sexual theory because this was the sole bulwark of reason against possible "eruption of the black flood of occultism." In these words Freud was expressing his conviction that the unconscious still harbored many things that might lend themselves to "occult" interpretation, as is in fact the case. These "archaic vestiges," or archetypal forms grounded on the instincts and giving expression to them, have a numinous quality that sometimes arouses fear. They are ineradicable, for they represent the ultimate foundation of the psyche itself. They cannot be grasped intellectually, and when one has destroyed one manifestation of them, they reappear in an altered form. It is this fear of the unconscious psyche which not only impedes self-knowledge but is the gravest obstacle to a wider understanding and knowledge of psychology. Often the fear is so great that one dares not admit it even to oneself.[cviii]

The Oedipus complex, Freud's most famous theory, is the central conflict of the human mind that leads to the creation of the *superego*. A fully formed *superego* consists of a conscience and ego-ideal (ideal self), which helps the *ego* control the *id* through feelings of guilt and pride. All the above said in words we can all understand: our conscience and an idealistic image of ourselves is created through the training we receive as children, and the rational self—the conscious part of us—is always trying to mediate between the idealistic self and the unrealistic desires of our instincts. To put it succinctly, it's Plato's horses all over again, but in this scenario reason takes the place of the will, making tradition the driver and the one force that should control us. And this is not an accident as Freud's observations give us a tantalizingly accurate picture of the inner struggles of Victorians as they faced the strict gender roles. Freud, being part of a patriarchal world, believed these gender roles were a necessary part of society and that by identifying with the parent of the same sex, children would become well-adjusted adults. And of course he was right as adjustment requires acceptance. Only by accepting their future roles would people be able to adjust to the strict gender roles of the Victorian world.[cix]

Even if we ignore the most obvious issues, what makes the Oedipus complex so hard to swallow is Freud's insistence women will never be able to develop their conscience to such a degree that they will be able to become mature adults. This is, of course, part and parcel of the patriarchal worldview that sees women as mentally weak and fickle. Freud defended his view by explaining if the Oedipus complex isn't resolved properly, the individual will experience neurosis and a maladjusted sexuality as the *superego* fails to project a healthy ego-ideal to the *ego*. This holds true of both boys and girls, although girls experience the Oedipus complex (or Electra complex as Carl Jung named it) as penis envy and a desire to have a child with the father as a compensation for her own lack of a penis. The mother is seen as the reason for the girl's castrated state that results in hostility from the girl. To successfully resolve the complex the girl must learn to rescind her hostility and identify with the mother. But because, according to Freud, penis envy can never be fully resolved, the girl's *superego* (which in a boy is formed out of the conflict and fear of castration) can never be fully formed. To conclude, because the girl can never become a man and possess all the powers thereof, her desire for a penis will always be thwarted. As a result, her *superego*, the part of the mind that helps the *ego* control *id* in a way that is socially acceptable, will have to continuously suppress the desires of *id* instead of allowing *ego* to enlarge and be where *id* once was. This continuous suppression causes women to fail to become psychologically mature persons as they experience continuous conflict. And this in turn is the reason for their need to be guided and controlled by men in accordance with patriarchal myth.

Talking about myth, as none of us create our theories in a vacuum, neither did Freud. Had *Rex Oedipus*, the famous Greek play, not been performed in Vienna during Freud's days and had the general mood of the entire society not been turned inwards looking for what's inside the human rather than outside the way the English did, had Freud ended up creating the Oedipus complex? Perhaps yes, but then, maybe not. Regardless, Freud's theory can rightly be seen as a handy way to explain the inferiority of women, for whereas the English and Americans talked about morally superior women to keep women from voting, Freud claimed women were morally deficient (echoing Darwin), perhaps in an effort to keep Austrian women from gaining the equal rights they were demanding.

Details notwithstanding, what is important for our purposes is Freud's claim the unsuccessful resolution of the Oedipus complex (phallic stage) and the two earlier stages (oral and anal) led to passive, aggressive, or vain behavior in men, and seductive or overtly submissive, and servile behavior in women. These are behavior patterns religious patriarchy claims occurs when people fail to adhere to strict religious moral codes. And it is only natural theologians would make such a claim, for their morality focuses on middle-class nuclear families and their proper formations in the likeness of Freud.[cx] But whereas Freud believed the key to helping his patients was a discharge of suppressed desires through psychoanalysis and an acceptance of cultural roles in order to avoid inner conflict, religious patriarchy believes the key to happiness is greater parental supervision during teen years and the rejection of desires and modern cultural roles — although the patriarchal ones offered *are* cultural roles. And so we find Freud and religious patriarchy to be bedfellows; odd ones, but bedfellows nevertheless.

Freud was rightly concerned about the repressed sexuality he observed in his Victorian patients, but despite his observations, even he would speak of morality — or the lack thereof — of certain sexual behaviors:

> We surely would not expect that these poor
> naked cannibals should be moral in their sex life
> according to our ideas, or that they should have
> imposed a high degree of restrictions upon their

sexual impulses. And yet we learn that they have considered it their duty to exercise the most searching care and the most painful rigour in guarding against incestuous sexual relations. In fact their whole social organization seems to serve this object or to have been brought into relation with its attainment... A few sentences from Frazer's book will show how seriously such trespasses are treated by these savages who are otherwise very immoral."[cxi]

Freud was making a value judgment based on his own culture and those rarely end well — calling someone a "savage" is hardly a scientific way to approach any people group. Naturally he was far from the only one who has ever considered a behavior pattern to be immoral simply because it is unfamiliar. As already noted, familiarity and morals are such close neighbors that you could pitch a tent over both and you wouldn't miss either. When he chose to make a value judgment instead of remaining neutral, Freud missed an opportunity to challenge his preconceived notions causing his confirmation bias to do the rest. Yet, although theories may be wrong — as they often are — observations are rarely wrong because our senses are honest.[cxii] Accordingly, Freud saw something other people wanted to ignore, but he didn't know what to do with the information, because it didn't fit the accepted cultural norms of his time. And since he didn't know what to do with the information, he created a theory that couldn't answer the questions he had set out to answer, although he did get the conversation started. All of this brings us to the question, what should we do about our suppressed thoughts and the guilt that follows?

While treating his patients, guilt seemed to have shown up everywhere Freud looked. According to Freud, individual guilt isn't the only thing working on our psyche; there is also something we all suffer from—a collective guilt. Freud's attempt to explain original sin and our collective feeling of guilt caused him to look for an answer in biology. Freud, following Darwin, believed the first humans lived in small groups in which the violent and controlling father kept all the women to himself, castrated his sons and kept them as workers or banished them. Freud concluded the younger men eventually rebelled, killed the father, instituted exogamy, and created bands of brotherhood around the totem. This killing of the original father, and the destruction of the patriarch, was recorded in the *id* to be experienced by every boy as the Oedipus complex—the desire to kill the father and sexually possess the mother.[cxiii] The successful resolution of the complex would allow the boy to identify with his father and transfer his love for his mother to another woman and thus avoid incest. It's a plausible explanation. Or, perhaps Freud recognized a very genuine abhorrence of patriarchy that is lodged deeply in our unconscious and that he couldn't explain without dismantling patriarchy itself. And perhaps it is this abhorrence of the ruling father that is suppressed when the child identifies with the parent of their own sex, believing they have successfully resolved the Oedipus complex and become healthy, well-adjusted grownups, all the while being trapped in the patriarchal world of stereotypes and endless suppression—and therefore, guilt.

But there was also another obsession at work in the background. We know Freud was disappointed in his father and that he loved his mother who always favored him above all her other children. He even went so far as to say the following in a lecture:

> A mother is only brought unlimited satisfaction by her relationship to a son; this is altogether the most perfect, the most free from ambivalence of all human relationships. A mother can transfer to her son the ambition which she has been obliged to suppress in herself, and she can expect from him the satisfaction of all that has been left over in her of her masculinity complex.[cxiv]

The fact that Victorian women had to live through their sons is nothing new, and some women still choose to do so in our days. According to Freud, it is how things should be, perhaps because of his own great love for his mother, although he made the following concession:

> That is all I had to say to you about femininity. It

is certainly incomplete and fragmentary and does not always sound friendly. But do not forget that I have only been describing women in so far as their nature is determined by their sexual function. It is true that that influence extends very far; but we do not overlook the fact that an individual woman may be a human being in other respects as well.[cxv]

Gee, thanks Freud.

Carl Jung, Freud's former disciple and student, rejected the Oedipus complex as he was determined to find what the unconscious was hiding and as a result, rid humanity from the harmful stereotypes that only hinder humanity's quest of discovering its own true self.

Since self-knowledge is a matter of getting to know the individual facts, theories are of very little help. For the more a theory lays claim to universal validity, the less capable it is of doing justice to the individual facts. Any theory based on experience is necessarily statistical; it formulates an ideal average which abolishes all exceptions at either end of the scale and replaces them by an abstract mean. This mean is quite valid, though it need not necessarily occur in reality. Despite this it figures in the theory as an unassailable fundamental fact.[cxvi]

Freud insisted all humans go through the same stages of development as children and cease to develop further in adulthood. This belief was rejected by Jung. He believed our minds continue to develop all of our lives and stereotypes only hurt and stunt our individual development. Perhaps Freud's insistence that the mind's development ends with childhood had to do with the body: if the body stops growing, why shouldn't the mind? Regardless of the answer, what is important here is that—in the likeness of Darwin—Freud was looking for a singular cause to all the neuroses he observed; if there is only one cause, all neuroses could easily be explained. Unfortunately for Freud, the mind isn't quite as easy to decipher as no two minds are exactly alike. And so we find that patriarchy has to insist on a rigid model, for if the mind is fluid, gender stereotypes are as suitable for the mind as oil is for water. In fact, we could go as far as to say that the one-size-fits all model is the *cause* of observable neuroses as the mind actively rejects this simplistic model.

One of the gender stereotypes our modern minds actively reject is the belief the man has superior reasoning ability compared to the woman. Historically the man ruled because of his greater physical strength. But as the power structures began to shift and shrewdness in politics became the new kingmaker, the belief in the man's superior reasoning ability took precedence over physical strength. I say belief, because although we have a clear visible manifestation of the man's physical strength, we lack similar proof of the man's much vaunted reason. As time went on, the man's physical body became less important, but the woman's physical appearance became the most important thing she could possess. In other words, intelligence became attractive in a man, but not in a woman.

The human body is beautiful. But although all bodies are beautiful, women's bodies are objects of incredible scrutiny. No matter how hard women work at perfecting their bodies they don't usually get even close to creating the ideal of the perfect female body, which leaves a lot of women feeling as abject failures. The question is, of course, why should women spend all their time and effort beautifying their faces and bodies when they could spend the time beautifying their minds? The answer is simple: patriarchy has to keep women occupied with things that are unimportant to keep them from discovering the truth that hides right behind the mud mask: every woman has a mind that is capable of thinking and deliberating. A woman who thinks for herself is formidable, and her looks are largely unimportant to her. People don't worry so much about what the mirror shows when they know their thoughts and actions are more important. When women are concerned with *how* they look rather than *who* they are, they become obsessed with their looks as their bodies are continuously on display for all to see. And this ties to the idea that men look for beautiful women because they like the status it brings. People buy art for the same reason. No one expects the art to do anything other than enhance the existence of its owner.

Already in 1792 the great feminist, Mary Wollstonecraft, wrote:

> Civilized women of the present century, with a few exceptions, are only anxious to inspire love, when they ought to cherish a nobler ambition, and by their abilities and virtues exact respect.[cxvii]

To inspire love young women had to dress like dolls and play house and forgo the life of the mind, because what mattered in a woman was youth and beauty.

> Why are girls told that they resemble angels; but to sink them below women? Or, that a gentle innocent female is an object that comes nearer to the idea which we have formed of angels than any other. Yet they are told, at the same time, that they are only like angels when they are young and beautiful; consequently, it is their persons, not their virtues, that produce them this homage.[cxviii]

The virtuous woman of obedience and beauty from

Shakespeare's *Shrew* became enshrined in the angelic doll whose existence revolved around pleasing a man with her childlike docility. But outward docility can also hide a mind as shrewd as that of Abigail who saved her household from her husband's imbecility, and as cunning as that of Herod's wife who had John the Baptist's head served on a platter.[cxix] Being fully aware of this truth, men who attempt to create docility in women also fear women who appear docile; a housecat hides its claws when purring, but it has claws nevertheless. When Schopenhauer said women lacked a sense of justice, he was making an accurate observation, but he failed to perceive the underlying cause.

> The fundamental defect of the female character is a lack of a sense of justice. This originates first and foremost in their want of rationality and capacity for reflexion but it is strengthened by the fact that, as the weaker sex, they are driven to rely not on force but on cunning... A completely truthful woman who does not practice dissimulation is perhaps an impossibility, which is why women see through the dissimulation of others so easily it is inadvisable to attempt it with them. – But this fundamental defect which I have said they possess, together with all that is associated with it, gives rise to falsity, unfaithfulness, treachery, ingratitude, etc. Women are guilty of perjury far more often than men. It is questionable whether

they ought to be allowed to take an oath at all.[cxx]

What women needed then, and still do, is the freedom to use their own minds in order to understand the precepts of justice and be held accountable for its demands instead of resorting to trickery (no one blames a cat for using its claws to defend itself, but women are blamed for using the only methods available to them). But there is also another reason why patriarchy insists women must focus on their looks at the exclusion of their minds: weakness of body is believed to imply weakness of mind, and this was already believed to be true by the old Romans:

> The weakness and light-mindedness of the female sex (*infirmitas sexus* and *levitas animi*) were the underlying principles of Roman legal theory that mandated all women to be under the custody of males.[cxxi]

Accordingly, John Chrysostom, bishop of the Eastern Roman city Constantinople, wrote:

> This had not been said to her before... The woman taught once, and ruined all. On this account therefore he said, let her not teach. But what is it to other women, that she suffered this? It certainly concerns them; for the sex is weak and fickle, and he is speaking of the sex collectively.[cxxii]

But if physical strength is connected to mental strength, why aren't physically weak men considered mentally weak? It's usually the other way around: the weaker the body, the stronger the mind. In other words, if the woman is physically weaker, should it not mean that her mind must be stronger? Here the old Victorian physicians rush in and explain to us the woman's womb makes her unfit for intellectual exertions:

> The conviction that women's subordinate position was biologically ordained had roots in antiquity, and it was a commonplace in nineteenth-century medical discussion to note that the womb exerted a supremely powerful force from which men were free. As one physician explained, it was as though the "Almighty, in creating the female sex, had taken the uterus and built a woman around it." The womb the doctors emphasized, dominated a woman's mental as well as physical life, producing a weak, submissive, uncreative, emotional, intuitive, and generally inferior personality.[cxxiii]

And so we find that the body dictates once again the destiny of everywoman and motherhood becomes the overarching reason why women shouldn't use their minds. The other reason is, unsurprisingly, sex.

Chapter 8

Body Politics

> "Sex, as one of the most intensive forms of relationships,
> Has turned into a prime commodity."
>
> *Marianne Katoppo*

Sex is a complicated subject, because it is tied to violence, love, procreation and recreation, in addition to money, honor, shame, and purity. Nothing about sex is simple, but neither is it so complicated that we cannot understand it as sex is a natural instinct and the body knows what it wants. What complicates matters is our tendency to see sex primarily as a moral issue. We look at sex through the lens of morality, because we (or I should say, those who believe in patriarchal morality) are convinced we have a moral responsibility to make sure everyone follows the same rules, the rules patriarchy has given us. As already noted, patriarchal morality insists sex is only acceptable when it happens within a heterosexual marriage. This is tied to the idea that a woman's body belongs to both a man *and* the community as her body is the source of children (for the community) and sex (for the man). Hence a woman's sexuality and her body must be strictly controlled, for what if she decides to do something other than marry and have children?

Even as women are guided into living their lives

through their bodies, they are told their bodies don't belong to them. All women in patriarchal societies learn early that their bodies belong to a man, and who that man is, is not up to them. While they sit in their fathers' houses and wait to be told who that man is, they aren't allowed to even consider another. To prevent temptation, some patriarchal societies cover women from head to toe; others use modesty rules and shaming tactics. Women themselves are expected to remain silent and accept their fate. If a woman *does* speak up, especially if she rejects the idea of being treated as a science project on how much control a person can handle without snapping, she is treated as an adversary. And depending on how patriarchal the society is, her community and family may be given the right to use any means available to subdue her and force her to obey the rules that were created without her input. Honor killing is perhaps the most visible manifestation of this principle, but what is this honor? It is the honor of denying opportunities through the threat of bodily harm. If women were allowed to make their own decisions, patriarchy's goal of controlling women in order to control men would be frustrated. Let me explain.

In the complex hierarchy (that includes class and race as factors) women get sandwiched between the controlling and the controlled men. A woman who stands up for her own rights disrupts the symmetry between the man as oppressor and the man as oppressed. The woman has no room in this symmetry because she is neither. She is seen as property and property simply is without understanding that it is. A human being understands its existence as a separate entity, but property isn't separate. Property has to by necessity belong to someone to *be* property; its whole existence depends on its relation to its owner, and it can be discarded at any moment as easily as it can be kept for a lifetime. And because women are considered property in patriarchal societies, all women are taught to accept the fact they must marry and become someone's wife, someone's property. As women they belong to men, and therefore their bodies belong to men. This in turn has huge ramifications as far as sex is concerned: sex can be a manifestation of love only when everyone is free. In the world of patriarchy freedom is a privilege given to men, making sex more or less a transaction, even (or especially) within marriage.

The need to control women's bodies isn't only about honor and hierarchy. The belief women's sexual behavior decides the destiny of entire societies is an ancient one. Edith Deen has this to say on the subject:

> The loss of energy, due to the relaxation of sexual standards, may not be immediately realized in the generation that first lets down the bars, says Unwin, but it shows up in the second and third generations afterward. Greater energy is maintained, according to his theory, so long as the mothers of new generations are reared in an environment of high ideals. "The Moors of Spain could never have advanced," he says, "had they not mated with women who had been reared in a more rigorous tradition than their own." The

quality of their wives helped create a more traditional culture. The Hebrews were the wisest of all, for they recorded in the Bible their laws regulating sexual standards. Although the rigorous laws in Leviticus and Deuteronomy are too often forgotten in the world today, they demanded then as now that men and women render perfect obedience to all the moral laws of God. These sexual laws are intermingled in the Bible with ceremonial laws in which there have been vast changes, but those laws dealing with moral behavior never change. Women then as now must be the standard-bearers of the race of sexual matters, which hold the clue to our weakness or our strength as a nation.[cxxiv]

Superstitious beliefs and magical thinking become part of a worldview in need of a reason for its rules in the absence of any defensible justification. The practice of blaming sexually active unmarried women when a society is weakened tells us the patriarchal ideal of virginity rests on a rather shaky ground for they used to think something similar during the witch craze when people were convinced young women were having intercourse with the devil when bad things happened. There is a certain kind of logic behind this line of thinking although it collapses under its own impossibility: why give men authority if young women can ruin it all by sleeping with the wrong man at the wrong time even if it's just once before the wedding night? Or perhaps it's the reason patriarchy insists on controlling women's bodies as their freedom would prove the patriarchal ideology to be nothing more than a house of cards as there is more to women than their bodies.

The patriarchal division of women into Madonnas and Whores (based on how their bodies are used) is found everywhere, and it is not so difficult to understand when we realize men want women to be both, but not at the same time. The Madonna part is easy to explain: every man wants a woman who will take care of him and give him children. The Whore part is a bit more complicated as men want women to be sexually provocative, but they want them to be *submissively* provocative. In other words, men want the permission to do what they wish to women, as seen vividly in pornography. And although men talk about how the only thing women have to do is to choose to be a "good" woman to stay safe, it betrays an underlying problem within patriarchy that is rarely talked about: the above division treats women only as objects or property as there is no opportunity for a woman to avoid becoming one or the other. There is no, "woman, a person" in this equation. The only choice a woman has is either to provoke and obey, or cover up and obey. It's Hobson's choice all over again. And it's done purposefully to prevent women from using their own power to equalize the equation.

The body as a source of power for women, while at the

same time being the source of their powerlessness, is deeply embedded in the patriarchal psyche. Women are expected to be beautiful, but since beauty gives women power, they are also expected to hide their beauty, much like men must hide the source of their own patriarchal power. One of the most striking features of modern patriarchy is the concealment of the penis, which during antiquity was proudly displayed in all public and private places as a sign of the man's dominance. Yet, it wasn't the penis itself that gave the man power, for if it did, even little boys would have the same power as grown men. It was what he could do with it that gave the man the power as sex was a method by which a freeborn man controlled both women and slaves; only the freeborn man was allowed to penetrate others as his body was considered inviolable. And this brings us to another historical curiosity. A Roman slave couldn't technically be raped as he was considered property; only the owner could sue for damages. Similarly a Victorian husband could sue a man who had assaulted his wife (or her lover), but the woman had no such recourse as she was considered a legal nonentity. This mentality caused rape to be an ever-present epidemic that wasn't addressed until the twentieth century when women became legal adults able to sue and be sued, and it ended the man's impunity to rape at will. And so we find the man's power to inflict pain through sexual violence is what his penis represents in patriarchy. And that explains perhaps why we now insist the penis needs to be hidden, as we no longer have an appetite for overt violence. The violence is still there, it's just hidden from view.

This thought leads us to consider clothing. Because women are expected to be beautiful, but not too beautiful to tempt a man, one of the dilemmas women have always faced is how to dress their bodies to avoid becoming objects of male lust. Religious patriarchy covers the whole woman and says it's a matter of respect; respect for the woman who avoids the male gaze, and respect for the man who avoids being tempted. Pornography undresses the whole woman and tells us a woman's body exists for the male gaze. But what if the problem isn't what women wear or don't wear? Maybe Jesus was right about plucking out the offending eye, for if clothing made a difference in how men view women's bodies, the army should have zero sexual assaults per year. The fact the army has a huge problem tells us clothing isn't the underlying cause of sexual assault. If a man will pick a woman from the row of identically dressed women, clearly he is looking for what's underneath, and no amount of clothing is going to prevent a man who views women's bodies as an open invitation from assaulting women.

Since everyone knows clothing has nothing to do with how men treat women, the division of women into Madonnas and Whores reinforces patriarchy's claim it provides a safety net for women who choose to obey a man in the confines of a home. But how great is this protection? If women must obey certain men to remain safe from other men they must by necessity remain in the home out of fear of becoming targets. And yet, one woman's protector is another woman's predator, not to mention when the protector turns against the woman he's supposed to protect. If the world isn't a safe place — as patriarchy insists — why do we assume men will make it safe for women? And so we find, once again, that patriarchy gives the man authority when he needs it the least, and removes the woman's agency and ability to protect herself when she needs it the most.

Augustine concluded the body as a source of powerlessness for the man (and the woman's power over the man) was seen in a man's inability to control his sexual impulses. He considered involuntary erections as a sign the body was the source of all evil, for perfection required the mind to control the body perfectly. This thought was not unique to Augustine. Plato's favorite complaint was the way senses trick the mind. To fix the problem he decided the body should be disregarded completely to allow the soul to live a bodiless existence. This led to a lopsided philosophy, which later caused an even more lopsided theology as the two merged in Augustine's voluminous works. The lopsidedness is clearly seen in how we view sex as a source of contamination and impurity, mostly because everything that has to do with procreation made one unclean in the laws found in the Hebrew Bible. The later meshing of ritual impurity with moral impurity made sex *the* cardinal sin of Christianity and the woman the cardinal sinner whose only hope of salvation is through the renunciation of her own self.

Woman the Sinner, Man the (almost) God

The defectiveness of women and the saintliness of men is a reoccurring theme in patriarchy, and it has to do with the old fear that women are always plotting the man's downfall if given even the smallest chance. Remember the old English law and how it dealt with a woman who murdered her husband? She was burned on the stake, a cruel and unusual punishment reserved for witches and heretics. The man could be executed or sent to prison if he killed his wife, but because he was simply dealing with his own property, if he killed his wife in response to her adultery, the charges were reduced to manslaughter.[cxxv] The church added its own toxic notion to the whole as seen in this quote from the founder of Latin Theology, Tertullian:

> If there dwelt upon earth a faith as great as is the reward of faith which is expected in the heavens, no one of you at all, best beloved sisters, from the time that she had first "known the Lord," and learned (the truth) concerning her own (that is, woman's) condition, would have desired too gladsome (not to say too ostentatious) a style of dress; so as not rather to go about in humble garb, and rather to affect meanness of appearance, walking about as Eve mourning and repentant, in order that by every garb of penitence she might the more fully expiate that which she derives from Eve, — the ignominy, I

mean, of the first sin, and the odium (attaching to her as the cause) of human perdition. "In pains and in anxieties dost thou bear (children), woman; and toward thine husband (is) thy inclination (conuersion), and he lords it over thee." And do you not know that you are (each) an Eve? The sentence of God on this sex of yours lives in this age: the guilt must of necessity live too. You are the devil's gateway: you are the unsealer of that (forbidden) tree: you are the first deserter of the divine law: you are she who persuaded him whom the devil was not valiant enough to attack. You destroyed so easily God's image, man. On account of your desert—that is, death—even the Son of God had to die.[cxxvi]

Deicide (murder of God) is perhaps the most severe indictment anyone can be accused of. Not only did the woman destroy the man, she tried to destroy God. Can anyone be more evil than that?

The belief the woman is intrinsically evil is linked to the woman's inferiority as this inferiority isn't only about the weakness of the mind; it is also about a general lack of goodness. Plato's answer to evil, the removal of the body, begged the question why the gods put humans in a body in the first place. Since there was no answer, other philosophers sought alternative answers to the question of evil. The Neo-Platonist Plotinus explained the existence of evil as an absence of goodness. In other words, that which is evil, instead of being a thing of its own, simply contains less goodness.[cxxvii] This lack of goodness is said to be caused by the inability of matter to perfectly replicate form. Accordingly, we find Aristotle believing the purpose of the existence of matter was to become perfected, and since he believed the male human represents the form of human perfectly, the woman was by necessity a less perfect human, "a misbegotten male," and possessed therefore less goodness. This rather unorthodox belief was due to his belief the semen is the active agent in the production of a human; the sperm produces the form, the womb produces only the matter, and since only the man can produce semen, only the man is able to be an active agent in the act of procreation, and therefore fully human. But Aristotle didn't stop there. He took the concept to its logical conclusion when he translated it to the realm of the mind: only the man is able to be an active agent in the matters of the mind; the woman's mind can only receive the man's words in the same way as her body receives the semen, and produce the matter, that is, her obedience.

If all of this seems confusing, it is simply, well, because it is. Modern science has debunked most of what Aristotle and his contemporaries said, but we still talk as if we're stuck in Aristotle's Lyceum. Feminism is considered a clear manifestation of the woman's attempt to control the man—as was witchcraft a few hundred years ago. The witch craze, that spanned three centuries from the Reformation to the Revolutionary period, was a time of intense violence against women. A few men were accused of witchcraft, but mostly the victims were women. One of the main tenets of the persecution of women was the belief women were in allegiance with the devil, that they cast love spells on men, hurt livestock and children, and caused famines. The old ideas from antiquity blended with (at that time) modern thoughts creating a unique kind of hysteria that sent an untold number women to their deaths. But as no story in our western world is written without a patriarchal backdrop, the persecution of women as witches had also a very distinctly economical angle to it. Anne Llewellyn Barstow explains:

> The spread of the capitalist system across western Europe during the sixteenth century markedly affected women's work and was a direct factor in the spread of witch accusations. Heidi Hartmann argues that capitalism grew on top of patriarchy and that the two became "inextricably intertwined." Early capitalism made the poor poorer because, in seeking the large pool of cheap labor that it required, it displaced farm families from their smallholdings, forcing them to become wage laborers. But it was men who had previously been the chief occasional wage earners; though they lost their land and independence to wealthy capitalist farmers, poor men still found work for wages. But women, who had supported themselves (and often their families) from their gardens and dairies, lost their main source of income, and they could not compete with men

for paid jobs. These were the conditions that plunged many single women, formerly self-supporting, into poverty in the period 1550 to 1700. The economic situation accounts for the alarming increase in female beggars in western Europe, who so discomfited their better-off neighbors that the neighbors accused them of witchcraft in order to get rid of them.[cxxviii]

The rise of capitalism as the economic arm of patriarchy coupled with religious anxiety caused a murderous rampage across the continent, and the laws of coverture would cause the economic situation of women to worsen. Thankfully the nineteenth-century response was one of legal reform instead of more bloodshed. But the idea of women's inherent defectiveness remained.

Even as modern women, we grow up believing our bodies belong to everyone else but ourselves. From childhood we have been taught to believe this idea that our value depends on our attractiveness; a plain girl grows up believing herself worth less than her more attractive sisters. Yet, being attractive is also a cause of shame, for we are told our bodies cause men to become tempted. We need to be pretty, but not too pretty; congenial, but not too congenial; in control, but obedient. The balance is impossible to find as there is none, and for a good reason: every woman is different, we aren't all the same. What works for some, doesn't work for others. But most of all, the middle doesn't exist because our bodies don't exist for other people.

Your body is yours

It doesn't belong to your parents, or your family, or society. Your body is not a political statement, or a history lesson. It is not there to make people happy. You live in your body; it belongs to you. And this is where the problem of catcalling comes in. Every woman has heard the prompt to smile in some form or the other. A woman can't even run for president without being told to smile.[cxxix] So why do men insist women should smile to perfect strangers they just met on the street?

> It's not about a legitimate need for women to be happy as much as it's that smiling/pleasant-looking women are easier on the eyes and more inviting to approach. It's really not about the woman at all. If you really are that hard-pressed for a woman to smile, tell a joke, slip on a banana peel, pay her phone bill; basically, instead of asking a stranger to fake an expression for you, do something that might legitimately brighten her day. Who knows, she might even smile. And, she might not. You have

no control over that, and that's kinda the point.[cxxx]

A man who catcalls isn't thinking about the woman; he is thinking about his own feelings, his need to see a pretty smile. Catcalling follows the same logic as pornography: it is something done to strangers without any regard to their personhood. A man doesn't catcall his best friend's daughter, or the CEO of the company he works for, nor does he expect to see his wife on the screen. But the same man will whistle after a stranger on the street; she is an easy target of unwanted attention that comes with no real consequences. Most women find catcalling annoying, yet it persists. But why is that? We've managed to stop people from smoking in public places, so why not catcalling and unwanted attention? The problem seems to be men don't agree telling strange women to smile is a problem. They think it's a compliment, something women should appreciate. After all, they are giving women attention, and that in itself is something all women should appreciate.

It's reasoning befitting a narcissist.

But before we begin to see flirting as something ugly, we need to remind ourselves attraction is a beautiful thing as love is a quintessential part of our universe and something to be appreciated. People are beautiful and being beautiful is not a crime, neither is admiring beauty as long as it's done in the right way and for the right reasons. But beauty can also become an idol, to be worshipped for its own sake. Evolutionists speak of beauty as a sign of health, but in our times we talk about beauty in terms of wealth. Sexual selection has been reduced to a caricature of its original intent as men seek power to gain access to beautiful women, and women seek beauty to gain access to wealth. It's as foolish as it sounds, and far too many novelists have gained their inspiration from real life tragedies as the dream turned into a nightmare. Money and power do not have the ability to create happiness; money especially is a harsh taskmaster: the more we have the more we need to protect it from threats—both real and imagined. And that makes every person we meet a suspect, and a potential enemy; "Does she smile because she likes me or because she likes my money?" A person, who is always protecting something he owns can never relax and be his authentic self. He must always be on guard and think the world is a dangerous place. And it's exactly what patriarchy wants us to believe as fear keeps it going.

Sex and women's bodies in general are part of the larger patriarchal concept that sees women as mentally passive. This doesn't mean that women aren't expected to do things; women do an enormous amount of things every day, but what they do isn't considered as important as the things done by men, and that's where the difference lies: housework and childrearing are considered the proper work of mentally passive women due to the monotonous and repetitive nature of the work. It would be ironic if it wasn't so infuriating: on the one hand women are told to be passive, only to have their passivity used against them as proof that they should be passive. At the same time, a woman who refuses to be passive is considered an aberration; or worse yet, she is accused of trying to be a man. And this leads us to consider an old saying that is still very much with us—

Men are active, women are passive

Yin-yang is about balance. Yang represents masculinity, spirit, heat, day, hardness, and activity. Yin represents femininity, matter, cold, night, softness, and passivity. But before we try to claim one is better than the other, we need to realize that Yang needs Yin: male and female need each other, heat and cool create the seasons, night and day exchange places without an argument, spirit without matter cannot be touched, softness without hardness is spineless, activity without rest cannot be sustained. It would also be a mistake to say one dominates the other. The sun is passive from our perspective, but we need the sun; the sun doesn't need us. And although passivity is considered a feminine principle, it doesn't mean that *women* are passive. Masculinity and femininity are cultural constructs and have little to do with real men and women.

The belief women are passive is a patriarchal myth found especially in the bedroom. It is often said the woman is passive in the sex act because she is the one being penetrated. The assumption that penetrating is a sign of domination is a lasting legacy of Roman Empire. The Roman man was believed to dominate those outside of the empire with a sword, and those within with his penis. As the woman doesn't have a penis, she cannot dominate and must therefore be a passive recipient. But all of this begs the question, why do we equate penetration with domination? When it comes to a sword the point is clear: the penetration of the blade kills you. But penetration with a penis gives the partner pleasure—as long as it is consensual. So why do we assume that they man dominates the woman in the sex act? The problem is the assumption empty space is completely passive and incapable of responding in any other way than with passive acceptance. However, the seemingly unimportant empty space is the means and source of life, creativity, and movement. Without empty space the earth would not revolve around the sun, the rays of the sun would not reach all of the earth, and we wouldn't be able to live. In other words, the empty space isn't there only to passively facilitate movement; it is filled with something we need—air, heat, and life.

This brings us back to the question of sex. The man can only dominate if his partner is unwilling to participate, which explains why patriarchy works hard to convince women they shouldn't enjoy sex; that they should be passive and view sex only as a duty. But just as with tango, it takes two to make love. Perhaps some men enjoy a passive sex partner, but the most rewarding experiences come when both participate equally in the act of bodily worship. Love requires after all that we give as much in return as we take. Sex that contains no love is lust, and lust doesn't take the other person into account; it sees people only as objects, and objects do not know how to love, which explains why love and marriage are so seldom found together in patriarchal societies.

Chapter 9

Marriage and Divorce

"Is not marriage an open question, when it is alleged,
From the beginning of the world,
That such as are in the institution wish to get out,
And such as are out wish to get in?"

Ralph Waldo Emerson

Patriarchy tells us marriage is *the* bond that gives us love while preventing lust as it promotes healthy family values. But while we are busy trying to get into this blessed union others are desperate to get out of it. But why is that? Why do find this bond so often turning into a form of bondage instead of being a source of happiness? It has mostly to do with the patriarchal insistence everyone has to marry regardless of whether marriage will make them happy or not. Patriarchal religion especially has a long and bleak history of perpetuating the myth of the happy nuclear family in the guise of God's will ever since the Reformation. Although far from the only culprit, it is difficult not to hold the church responsible for all the abuses its teachings have perpetuated, especially when it comes to the near complete ban on divorce. And yet, evil cannot completely wipe out goodness. In some ways the church has helped create a better understanding of marriage we couldn't have formed without the help of the mystical meaning of Christ and the Church.[cxxxi] It is however also true that our current understanding of marriage as a symbol of Christ and the Church needs to be greatly reformed as it no longer represents its original intent. Carl Jung had this to say about the subject:

> This is not to say that Christianity is finished. I am, on the contrary, convinced that it is not Christianity, but our conception and interpretation of it that has become antiquated in face of the present world situation. The Christian symbol is a living thing that carries in itself the seeds of further development. It can go on developing; it depends only on us, whether we can make up our minds to meditate again, and more thoroughly, on the Christian premises. This requires a very different attitude towards the individual, towards the microcosm of the self, from the one we have adopted hitherto.[cxxxii]

The individual gets lost in the sea of theological arguments about the meaning of church and our place in it. It is as if the individual can only be understood as a peg that must be shoved into the right hole, or in the case of the Christian, stuffed into the right pew. The individual has no other role, because the church isn't understood as a living entity, but rather as a building. And because the church is seen as a building, the people are seen as inconsequential; an individual can be discarded at any time.

This relative unimportance of people is clearly seen in how we deal with marriage and divorce. Because the institution of marriage is considered to be far more important than the people who are married there is a general reluctance to grant a divorce. And this is of course exactly how patriarchy likes it, for if women are given the opportunity to initiate divorce, the man's authority would be rather pointless. If divorce is denied, women have no other option but to remain married regardless of what happens to them. But the question of divorce is complicated also by the fact there is no one answer that fits every generation that we can lean on, for as Augustine pointed out, customs are different in different times.[cxxxiii] In the Mosaic Law the continuation of family, tribe, and nation were in view, and very little was said about love, as marriage was an economic arrangement intended to facilitate the multiplication of people; divorce was a male prerogative. The prophets changed our understanding of marriage by adding love as a requirement, just as they changed our view on resurrection, also absent from the Law. Jesus talked about marriage as an original bond, but he allowed both men and women to seek divorce in case of *porneia* (the meaning of the Greek word has been hotly debated ever since). The early church, holding on to a general belief in the imminent return of Christ, prescribed perpetual celibacy for everyone rather than marriage; divorce was strictly forbidden. But as time went on and nothing happened, the church had to re-evaluate its ideas about marriage and divorce, and the natural place to look for inspiration was the surrounding society and the customs people were already used to.

> Through a gradual process, which was sometimes fully incarnational and sometimes merely symbiotic, Western cultural practices naturally shaped the structure of Christian marriage, even as these practices were themselves being influenced by the Christian message. "Thus down to the end of the fifth century in the West marriages were still celebrated in Christian families with some of the forms customary in pagan times, and the nuptial rite prescribed by Pope Nicholas I in the ninth century was that in use in imperial Rome with the substitution of the Mass for the pagan sacrifice. The use of the ring, for example, as a symbol of betrothal, and later as a sign of the contract, comes directly from pre-Christian Roman practice. From this same source comes also the Church's official formulation of the purposes of marriage: "in order to bring forth children."... It is not surprising, therefore, that "Canon Law's basic principles and obligations of the marriage contract seem to be similar to, if not identical with, Roman Law."[cxxxiv]

Just as Greece formed our understanding what our homes should look like, Rome gave us the model for marriage, and Christianity would continue to shape our ideas about marriage over the centuries until all the conflicting ideas were packed into one neat romantic product that became highly profitable as princess stories were added as a staple to little girls' bedtime stories; more than one four-year-old who grew up reading about Cinderella has ended up getting married looking just like Cinderella. But before we get too excited about the prospect of a fairytale romance, these real life brides get to spend an entire life in the reverse role as the original Cinderella, the ash child, cleaning and scrubbing while dreaming of the ball that once was and is no more. Patriarchy has no other plan for them, for although family is where we are taken care of, the patriarchal family doesn't take care of all of us equally as explained by Chodorow:

> Most theoretical accounts agree that women as wives and mothers reproduce people — physically in their housework and child care, psychologically in their emotional support of husbands and their maternal relation to sons and daughters. If we accept this view, we have to ask who reproduces wives and mothers. What is hidden in most accounts of the family is that women reproduce themselves through their own daily housework. What is also often hidden, in generalizations about the family as an emotional refuge, is that in the family as it is currently constituted no one supports and reconstitutes women affectively and emotionally — either women working in the home or women working

in the paid labor force. This was not always the case. In a previous period, and still in some stable working-class and ethnic communities, women did support themselves emotionally by supporting and reconstituting one another. However, in the current period of high mobility and familial isolation, this support is largely removed, and there is little institutionalized daily emotional reconstitution of mothers. What there is depends on the accidents of a particular marriage, and not on the carrying out of an institutionalized support role.[cxxxv]

These "accidents of a particular marriage" are the reason why the patriarchal marriage exacts such high price from women: their emotional health depends entirely on the character of their husbands; there is no built-in protective mechanism that will protect a woman in case her husband decides to turn against her or expect her to do all the work. On the other hand, when we separate marriage from family, marriage becomes a personal relationship between two equals who may or may not have children, and family becomes a generic term for the emotional and physical care of people that is done by various people in various ways. As a result of this separation, mothering is no longer exclusively women's work, and housework becomes everyone's business as everyone is either being cared for or caring for others. All of this has a profound implication on how we arrange our lives and how we view feminism. If women aren't born to marry and have children, clearly they are meant to do other things too, the things men have always done, the things *people* should be doing and have done. And it's not such a strange idea when we remember women are people too.

As with all the other aspects that have to do with patriarchy, the old Roman model of marriage adopted by Christians had a lot to do with money and class:

> Much of what is claimed as distinctively "Christian" in the morality of the early churches was in reality the distinctive morality of a different segment of Roman society from those we know from the literature of the wellborn. It was the morality of the socially vulnerable. In modestly well-to-do households the mere show of power was not available to control one's slaves or womenfolk. As a result, concern for intimate order, for intimate restraints on behavior, for fidelity between spouses and obedience within the household acted out "in singleness of heart, fearing God," tended to be that much more acute. Obedience on the part of servants, fair dealings between partners, and the fidelity of spouses counted for far more among

men more liable to be fatally injured by sexual infidelity, by trickery, and by the insubordination of their few household slaves than were the truly wealthy and powerful.[cxxxvi]

Those who wielded power and authority through wealth had no need to consider the feelings of those they controlled as the departure of their subjects didn't diminish their ability to survive; there were always other wives and slaves to be found. But those who depended on the labor of others had to ensure their spouses and slaves stayed. And so we find the strict divorce laws of early Christians were formed due to the naked facts of a harsh economy more than morals and became therefore a hindrance rather than a help as the economy improved.

As we've already found out, money shows up in the most awkward places in the patriarchal narrative. Just like in ancient Rome, love played a minimal role in the marriage arrangements created in the post-medieval society as people married to secure their financial futures, not their personal happiness. And who could blame them when money was scarcer than croup, and poverty was widespread. But the habit of choosing money over affection became too obvious when money ceased being such a rare commodity. Suddenly everyone talked about love and how they were going to do everything in their power to make their intended spouse happy. Talks about money became crass and vulgar; only true love was a good enough reason for marriage.

Modern western people hold on to both thoughts as

people are told to look for love—and money (although few will confess to such calculations). In addition, modern marriage is also a contradiction in terms as it supposedly begins with love that needs no contract, yet this love must be safeguarded and perpetuated through a contract. It is of course just our modern way of looking at things. The old Romans didn't sign contracts or require love. Marriage may have been mandatory for them, but it was as easy to exit as it was to enter—people could return from a trip to the countryside to find themselves divorced in their absence. So what caused our modern marriage to become such a peculiar combination of little bit of everything?

Modern marriage as a combination of love and a legal (patriarchal) contract is the result of the church having taken over the administration of wedding vows and the related questions of divorce and separation in the eleventh century (which explains King Henry VIII's "Great Matter" five centuries later). As the church took over, theologians began to earnestly discuss the meaning of marriage to enable to church do its work. As a result, marriage was changed from a family matter to a matter of individual consent in the twelfth century, and this seems to have created the contradictions we are dealing with today.

> The Canonist and Scholastic learning that came in with the eleventh century took up the lead given by Roman Law, which was then undergoing a kind of renaissance, and by Pope Nicholas I. Since the time of Ivo of Chartres (d.

1117), it insisted with increasing sharpness upon the distinction between an intention to marry directed to the present, and one directed to the future, on the part of the prospective partners. In the former (consensus de praesenti) one can clearly discern the motive that lies at the basis of marriage. In the teaching of Peter Lombard (d. 1160) "the Sponsalien distinktion became the foundation of a completely self-contained scholastic doctrinal system." And this does not only apply to the legal aspect. Peter Lombard was the first theologian to fix the seven sacraments. He stresses in the Sentences that it is exclusively the "consent" — the willing assent of both partners — that constitutes marriage (IV, 24, 2;PL 192, 915).… All that the reformers of the ninth century had stressed as particularly important — the orderly conclusion of the marriage contract, the wooing of the bride by the relatives, the betrothal, the dowry, the priestly blessing and the public wedding — all this is brushed aside as meaningless. He admits that it serves to increase the outward show and respectability of the marriage, but it is not essential for the validity of the sacramental marriage bond. Only the secretly given consent, he holds, constitutes a sacramental marriage, even if secret matrimony remained unlawful. This means for one thing that the sacramental

> bond of marriage is only accomplished through the recognizably expressed and willed decision of the prospective couple. It might almost be said, then, that husband and wife administer the sacrament to themselves and to their partner.[cxxxvii]

The importance of consent mirrors the view of conversion as an individual decision done secretly with God and baptism as the outward manifestation of this private union; baptism doesn't make the person a Christian, the new birth is affected by the Spirit in secret. Similarly, consent and willingness to be joined in marriage constitutes the marriage, not the ceremony; just as the Christian life and its validity is tested by the life of the believer, so is the validity of the marriage tested by the life of the married couple. Both can be declared invalid.

The patriarchal marriage ceremony and the giving of the bride to the groom by the father stresses the contract and familial ties far more than the consent of the couple and creates problems when divorce becomes an imminent reality: if the contract is more important than consent there is really no legal reason to break the contract other than adultery.[cxxxviii] But if consent is *the* essence of marriage, the lack of consent becomes a reason for divorce, which makes the Catholic refusal to grant a divorce in such cases rather strange.

The reason the Catholic teachings on marriage and divorce are so dissimilar is largely due to Augustine and his belief marriage is an impossibility in our world. Because Augustine believed the marriage unity could only become a reality in the Kingdom of God (or in the City of God, as he called it) he considered marriage to be an allowance due to the weakness of the flesh. But this begs the question, why did Augustine prohibit the dissolution of a bond that he didn't believe could exist on earth in the first place?

> Augustine has offered here a fascinating account of the relativity of moral standards based on the notion that sexual conduct can have different meanings (different "sacraments") in different periods of salvation history. For Augustine, the primary sacrament of marriages in the Hebrew Bible was their very multiplicity, a multiplicity that was fulfilled historically in the spread of Christianity throughout the world. In Christian times, by contrast, the primary sacrament in marriage is an indissoluble unity, a unity that will be realized only at the end of time in the City of God. As Augustine put it: "Out of many souls there will arise a city of people with a single soul and a single heart turned to God. This perfection of our unity will come about only after this pilgrimage [on earth], when no longer will anyone's thoughts be hidden from another, and no longer will anyone be in conflict with anyone about anything."[cxxxix]

Conflict avoidance and the maintenance of the Roman order were the main reasons why Augustine believed the marriage bond was impossible. Perhaps he was right seeing how few marriages survive the love-killing stress the patriarchal world creates and throws at us with enviable regularity. But there was also another more pressing reason: a general belief in negative privacy.

> What emerged from these centuries of anxious concern for the solidarity of a threatened group was a sharp negative sense of the private. What was most private on the individual, his or her most hidden feelings and motivations, those springs of and motivations, those springs of action that remained impenetrable to the group, "the thoughts of the heart," were looked to with particular attention as the possible source of the tensions that threatened to cause fissures in the ideal solidarity of the religious community. This was a distinctive model of the human being. The starting point was the heart, presented as a core motivation, reflection, and imagined intentions, that should ideally be single, simple — translucent to the demands of God and its neighbors. The double-hearted cut themselves of from God and their neighbors by retiring into those treacherous zones of negative privacy that screened them from such demands. Hence the sharpened features of the relations of the Jew, and later of the Christian, to the supernatural world. Shielded by "negative privacy" from the

eyes of men, the heart was held to be totally public to the gaze of God and His angels: "When one commits a transgression in secret, it is as though he has thrust aside the feet of the Divine Presence."[cxl]

Augustine was concerned about the lack of transparency as he believed without transparency there could be no unity. But there was also the question about control. One of the most common ways to control women is to make them feel ashamed for wanting a life of their own instead of accepting their role as wives and mothers. The fear of negative privacy that became part of the Christian idealism demanded complete transparency and the feeling of shame that followed any individualistic thought was designed to create cohesion within the group by reducing selfish thinking and behavior as shame created internal behavior modifications that caused people to adhere to the standards accepted by the group. At the same time, the standards were designed to create different behavior patterns in different members of the group, and the feeling of shame that made people feel they were different prevented them from objecting when they were treated differently, and this in turn created group cohesion, but at the expense of those who were made to feel they were inferior and worth less. Since Augustine didn't reject the husband's control over his wife (or the slaves), his fear of negative privacy must have been caused by a man's inability to read his wife's mind; men have always worried what women *really* think behind those plastic and pleasing smiles. Until the day when all secrets are revealed, Augustine thought it best not to marry at all.

Let's stop here to consider a global perspective for a moment. The fear of negative privacy is also found in Indian culture as the question how the individual fits in the community and how the community affects the individual is one that all cultures struggle with.

> Although it is important to recognize that societies may construct quite different conceptions of the individual and of selfhood from one and another and may, therefore, select from the range of human potential different qualities for emphasis, it is also important not to overdraw the distinctions. Western "egocentric" individuals must also be capable of becoming social beings; they can never be totally autonomous and independent of others. Reciprocally, non-Western "sociocentric" individuals cannot be totally interdependent and other-oriented. They must be capable of at least some autonomous thought and action. Interdependence-independence might best be conceptualized as a continuum along which

cultures fall according to the particular mixture of collectivist and individualist elements that they exhibit at any one time. One must, however, always remember that the effort to characterize such societal orientations requires building models with which to examine the actual behavior that different members of a society exhibit. In these two models it is, in fact, the tension between the two different constructions of self that often becomes culturally salient. In the West, for example, in Euro-American culture individuals are expected to be capable of independent action but also to be able to form stable and intimate emotional bonds with other – a pre-requisite for establishing nuclear families. There is a culturally formulated tension between "selfish individualism" and "mature individualism." In Hindu culture, in contrast, the tension is between the "selfish desires" of the individual and the interests of the joint family. Renunciation of personal desire is therefore culturally lauded and elaborated. As Mrs. Misra so poignantly pointed out, there are differences among Indian families and the degree to which individuals act morally where what is "moral" is culturally defined as giving precedence to family obligations over personal interests.[cxli]

For our purposes it is worth noting that where the individual has to fit in a stereotypical model society has formed for her, the renunciation of personal desires has to do mostly with the body: 1) some must become slaves because labor is hard and profits are minimal; 2) women must have children because the family has to be perpetuated. And it all makes sense in a world of scarcity, but as soon as prosperity arrives, the austerity measures no longer make sense, and scarcity must be artificially created to enforce the old model that no longer makes sense.

Perhaps all of the above was in Plato's mind when he created his philosophy and argued against the passions with a passion rarely seen before or after his time. We know Augustine was a great fan of Plato's philosophy, and because Plato regarded the body as intrinsically evil, as its demands made the world unjust, in Augustine's theology the woman becomes evil as the Bible compares the married woman to the body and the married man to the head in the famous Pauline analogy found in Ephesians 5. Strangely Augustine went back and forth, arguing the woman should/shouldn't be likened to the "flesh" (the part in us that causes us to sin), the man should be likened to the spirit (although the Bible likens the man to a head), that also women are holy (although punished with subjection to the man as a result of Eve's sin), and so on. As with most patriarchal reasoning, Augustine tried to affirm what he denied and it led to a rather odd theology that treated sex within marriage as a concession to the flesh rather than a physical expression of love. As a result of all of this, for more than a thousand years laypeople and theologians alike treated sex as a dirty little secret, until the sexual revolution returned sex to humanity by re-claiming it as a normal biological function, and a fun one at that. But since marriage isn't just about sex, the problem of divorce remained.

As noted above, the desertion of a dependent spouse was a major problem in the Roman world, and it still is in many parts of the world. The indissolubility of marriage became a defense against the cruel practice, but it placed people also in situations where they couldn't escape abusive or loveless marriages. When we look at the reason for the indissolubility of marriage in Catholic theology, we find a major flaw in the reasoning why the church chose to adopt such a harsh approach:

> If the contract is the sacrament by its very judicial nature and its juridical evidence, then it is relatively easy to control the validity of sacraments by marriage tribunals. If, however, the sacramental reality is the visibility of the gracious presence of Christ in the common striving of the spouses for ever greater love for each other, in the dedication to fidelity even to the point of redeeming the other from infidelity through generous forgiveness and reconciliation, and in the gracious "yes" to the mission of

fatherhood and motherhood, then a very different picture emerges. The covenant aspect then comes to the foreground. The good of the persons, their capacity to love, the fostering of conditions that favor their growth in love, the experience of redemption and redeeming love, the readiness to forgive: all this will be the main interest of the Church. But then — unfortunately — it will be much more difficult to determine the validity or non-validity of a marriage. Then also, the question of whether an existing marriage can be saved or not cannot so easily be ignored. How can we then so easily declare a marriage "invalid" which has all the signs of hope for working out as a covenant, and declare a marriage "valid" which no longer exists and cannot in any way be raised from death, and which from the very beginning gave little hope, from an anthropological point of view, that it could ever become a visible sign of the covenant between Christ and the Church?[cxlii]

The relationship between Christ and church is not contractual, it is covenantal, and a covenant requires mental assent, loyalty, and fidelity; it requires the spirit instead of just the letter of the law. Accordingly, the biblical covenant of marriage requires love and fidelity to be valid, and as such it comes with a different set of rules that allows for its dissolution when one, or both parties, have ceased to adhere to the requirements of the covenant. It is for this very reason idolatry is considered adultery in the Bible (as it transfers love and devotion to another) and God divorced Israel because of her idolatry.[cxliii] In James 4, also the church is called adulterous for favoring the rich over the poor and loving money more than God, as greed is considered idolatry.[cxliv]

> What causes fights and quarrels among you? Don't they come from your desires that battle within you? You desire but do not have, so you kill. You covet but you cannot get what you want, so you quarrel and fight. You do not have because you do not ask God. When you ask, you do not receive, because you ask with wrong motives, that you may spend what you get on your pleasures. You adulterous people, don't you know that friendship with the world means enmity against God? Therefore, anyone who chooses to be a friend of the world becomes an enemy of God.[cxlv]

Partnership with those who are greedy is not the only way to end our relationship with God as any of the individual members of the body of Christ can lose their connection with the head — Christ — due to pride.

> Do not let anyone who delights in false humility and the worship of angels disqualify you. Such a person also goes into great detail about what they have seen; they are puffed up with idle

notions by their unspiritual mind. They have lost connection with the head, from whom the whole body, supported and held together by its ligaments and sinews, grows as God causes it to grow.[cxlvi]

The unspiritual mind leads us to believe we are worth more than others. As a stark contrast, the spiritual mind is humble and considers also the interests of others.[cxlvii] For the members to remain connected to the head they must exhibit humility and care for the other members of the body, as our love for God is proven through our love for others.[cxlviii] Christian marriages are meant to mirror the relationship that exists between Christ and church. If we need humility to remain connected to Christ, can we really say we do not need humility to remain connected to our spouses?

All of this may sound like a bunch meaningless Bible talk, but it has a direct bearing on the subject of marriage as our understanding of marriage has been defined by the church for nearly a millennium. This brings us to the question how we should properly define humility as religious patriarchy insists it is women's refusal to obey men that is the clearest evidence of pride. But even Jesus didn't consider the right to command something to be grasped at.[cxlix] He gave up his power in order to become a servant, and servants don't have authority, they serve by virtue of their position. Yet, for some reason men demand to be served by women, especially the women they are married to, and it is considered to be right and proper by religious patriarchy. From a biblical perspective it is a sign of pride, and pride is what separates us from the life of God, for we are all created to serve one another through love. And it couldn't be any other way, for God is love.[cl]

Before we move on to consider the meaning of marriage in more detail, we need to talk a little bit more about the theology that lies right beneath the surface, so bear with me just for a little bit longer. For those who aren't familiar with the New Testament, a man named Paul wrote a bunch of letters to his friends while he was imprisoned due to his faith. A lot of these letters are named by the cities the letters were sent to, e.g., Galatians, Corinthians, Romans, etc. Two of these letters, Colossians and Ephesians, are twin letters. Ephesians is a bit longer and more detailed while Colossians talks more about the heavenly realm, but the focus of both letter is still the same—the relationship between the Church (the body) and Christ (the head). As this relationship is the foundation of Christian marriage, and since there is a general belief marriage is about authority, we need to take a closer look at these letters to see if there is something we have missed.

Earthly marriage is often seen as consisting of authority, sex, and procreation, and it is customary to point out earthly masters had the right to command their slaves and the slaves had a duty to obey, just as the husband had authority over his wife in ancient Rome. But this analogy breaks at the point where it appears the strongest: the wife is not a slave, although the law of coverture had as its foundation the old feudal laws and the relationship between Lord and peasant. This truth is captured succinctly by Lawrence G. Wrenn:

> We must come soon to the realization that it is the bond, not the bondage, that is important, that if we are genuinely interested in making marriage less dissoluble, then the most effective way to do that is not to insist on the bondage of marriage but to strengthen its bonds.[cli]

Because the instructions to the married in Ephesians 5 are followed by instructions to children and to slaves, it is customary to think of marriage and family being one and the same, the way Aristotle envisioned it. But what is usually ignored in this context is that the instructions to the married are preceded by instructions to *all* Christians, yet no one claims that the neighbor who sits next to you in church on Sunday is part of your family for that reason. And this leads us to consider something we've already noted: marriage and family is not the same thing. They can exist in the same place at the same time, but they are not the same. This distinction is especially important if we are going to understand God as a parent and us as co-creators with God the Spirit in bringing spiritual children into the world. They must be understood as separate entities. Especially as the purpose of the church as a bride of Christ is not procreation; it's love. We love Christ as

Christ loves us and it is this love that creates the unity we lacked before our union with Christ.[clii] This brings us to our second thought: if the purpose of the union of Christ and Church is love, it must also be the purpose of earthly marriage or the analogy in Ephesians 5 fails. Let's take a look at what Ephesians 5 has to say on the subject:

> Submit to one another out of reverence for Christ. Wives, submit yourselves to your own husbands as you do to the Lord. For the husband is the head of the wife as Christ is the head of the church, his body, of which he is the Savior. Now as the church submits to Christ, so also wives should submit to their husbands in everything. Husbands, love your wives, just as Christ loved the church and gave himself up for her to make her holy, cleansing her by the washing with water through the word, and to present her to himself as a radiant church, without stain or wrinkle or any other blemish, but holy and blameless. In this same way, husbands ought to love their wives as their own bodies. He who loves his wife loves himself. After all, no one ever hated their own body, but they feed and care for their body, just as Christ does the church — for we are members of his body. "For this reason a man will leave his father and mother and be united to his wife, and the two will become one flesh." This is a profound

mystery—but I am talking about Christ and the church. However, each one of you also must love his wife as he loves himself, and the wife must respect her husband.[cliii]

Did you count how many times the above text talks about love? Did you get six times? Love is a really important ingredient in Christian marriage and it makes perfect sense as the relationship between Christ and Church is one of love. So why do we think marriage has something to do with authority?

The idea marriage has to do with authority was created out of the words *kephale* ("head") and *hupotasso* ("submit"). These two words have traditionally been understood to mean authority and obedience, but the trouble with the idea is the Greek word *kephale* doesn't contain the idea of authority. It's simply the word for a literal head of a literal body when the words *kephale* ("head") and *soma* ("body") are present together; when we put both Greek words—head and body—together, we get a single entity, a human being. When the head is separated from the body the human dies; similarly a marriage dies when the husband (head) and the wife (the body) are separated.

It is here we find a biblical reason for divorce: just as a body without a head is dead, so is a marriage without love. Naturally God has the power and ability to resurrect a dead body, and therefore there is always the possibility for reconciliation and an affirmation of a true Christian marriage, but the burden of reconciliation rests on the spouse who refuses to love. Reconciliation should never be sought at the expense of the injured party as Christian teaching distinctly and specifically prohibits the injuring of an already injured person as evidenced in the parable of the Good Samaritan. Rather than walking away and wishing people well, the church must protect those who have been injured and provide for their healing. And although emotional trauma is difficult to prove, the church is not allowed to ignore the evidence when presented, and in no cases should the church compel the injured party to return to a marriage that is not only hurtful for the individual, but also hurts the church *en toto*, as the church is one body and if one member suffers, all of the members suffer.[cliv] To conclude, a Christian marriage should not hide abuse, nor should the church allow for its existence within the Body of Christ. The duty of all Christians is to expose the deeds of darkness, to bring them to the light.

All of the above begs the question, why does Ephesians 5 emphasize cooperation (*huptasso* means "to cooperate") rather than love when the text moves from mutual submission to married women? It all comes down to how our patriarchal societies are arranged and how specific gender stereotypes force us to behave: powerful men resort to violence and threats, while powerless women resort to trickery to get what they want and need (as we've already found out). What is the cure for these two ills? According to the Bible it's cooperation and selfless love. And this brings us back to Ephesians 5. Its advice is only needed in patriarchal societies where women are legally disadvantaged and where women are tempted to use trickery to get what they need; hence the Christian advice for married women to choose respectful and truthful cooperation over unjust behavior models. We know this to be the case from what the rest of the letter to the Ephesians says:

> Be completely humble and gentle; be patient, bearing with one another in love. Make every effort to keep the unity of the Spirit through the bond of peace. ... Be kind and compassionate to one another, forgiving each other, just as in Christ God forgave you. Follow God's example, therefore, as dearly loved children and walk in the way of love, just as Christ loved us and gave himself up for us as a fragrant offering and sacrifice to God. ... Therefore each of you must put off falsehood and speak truthfully to your neighbor, for we are all members of one body.[clv]

Married Christians are in no way different from other Christians; the same rules apply to everyone. Also husbands are instructed to be humble, gentle, patient, bearing with their wives in love in order to keep the unity of the Spirit through the bond of peace instead of resorting to violence and threats. Nowhere in sight is the heavy-handed law of coverture that gave married men near absolute power over their wives, for the humble do not command; they love.

Humility is essential as power makes people less sensitive to the needs of others and insensitivity is perhaps the greatest of all insults men have heaped on women if all the collective complaints from the past centuries are allowed to tell their tale. Having someone obey us makes us feel powerful, but power makes us also feel less empathetic towards other people because commanding gives us the same feeling of euphoria as love—without the sacrifice. In other words, power makes us feel less emotionally connected to other people, and this may be a great asset in situations in which emotions would be in the way, such as when we're performing a surgery or in the middle of a natural disaster. But when it comes to intimate human relationships, power gets only in the way as human relationships require a lot of empathy and sympathy, i.e., feeling what other people feel. Power removes this ability as power causes us to be only concerned with the one who has the power—ourselves. Love on the other hand willingly gives more than it gets in return. It is not motivated by what it gets, but by what it can give. And this is why the patriarchal model of marriage as the locus of authority, sex, and procreation doesn't fit with the biblical narrative that focuses on unity, love, and mutual submission.

One of the oldest and longest standing arguments against divorce is the concept a married couple becomes "one flesh" and Jesus is cited as the authority on the subject:

> "It was because your hearts were hard that
> Moses wrote you this law," Jesus replied. "But at
> the beginning of creation God 'made them male

and female.' For this reason a man will leave his father and mother and be united to his wife, and the two will become one flesh.' So they are no longer two, but one flesh. Therefore what God has joined together, let no one separate.clvi

The "beginning" that is mentioned here refers to the Book of Genesis:

> But for Adam no suitable helper was found. So the LORD God caused the man to fall into a deep sleep; and while he was sleeping, he took one of the man's ribs and then closed up the place with flesh. Then the LORD God made a woman from the rib he had taken out of the man, and he brought her to the man. The man said, "This is now bone of my bones and flesh of my flesh; she shall be called 'woman,' for she was taken out of man." That is why a man leaves his father and mother and is united to his wife, and they become one flesh.clvii

The phrase "bone of my bones and flesh of my flesh" is an important one, because it is connected to the "one flesh" that follows. In the book named after Prophet Samuel we find the following:

> And king David sent to Zadok and to Abiathar the priests, saying, Speak unto the elders of Judah, saying, Why are ye the last to bring the

> king back to his house? seeing the speech of all
> Israel is come to the king, even to his
> house. Ye are my brethren, ye are my bones and
> my flesh: wherefore then are ye the last to bring
> back the king?[clviii]

Because David shared the same origin with all the other
Israelites they were considered "one flesh" as each of them
was a piece from a larger chunk of flesh (to put it somewhat
morbidly).[clix] In fact, theologically speaking, all humanity is
"one flesh" as we all find our origin in the first man's flesh
and bones through the first woman.[clx] Just as God is one (there
is only one God) and many (God is Trinity), we are one
humanity and yet many individuals—one flesh, many bones.

In the text from the Gospel of Mark, Jesus adds the
word "two" to the original—the *two* become one flesh. It
doesn't mean only married people are "one flesh"; it means
marriage is possible because everyone is "one flesh." This
thought has huge ramifications to our understanding of
marriage and its meaning. In a striking move, The New
International Version (NIV) omits the phrase "of his flesh and
of his bones" found in the Greek in verse 30 of Ephesians 5.

> He who loves his wife loves himself. After all, no
> one ever hated their own body, but they feed
> and care for their body, just as Christ does the
> church— for we are members of his body [**of his
> flesh and of his bones**]. "For this reason a man
> will leave his father and mother and be united to
> his wife, and the two will become one flesh."

> This is a profound mystery—but I am talking
> about Christ and the church. However, each one
> of you also must love his wife as he loves
> himself, and the wife must respect her husband.[clxi]

If we are of the flesh and the bones of Christ, it has to mean
we are *like* Christ, just as Eve was *like* Adam, because she was
his flesh and bones; she was another human ("strange flesh"
(*heteras*) stands in opposition to "one flesh"). And since we are
in the likeness of Christ, the only likeness we could have
attained is that of holiness.

> Husbands, love your wives, just as Christ loved
> the church and gave himself up for her to make
> her holy, cleansing her by the washing with
> water through the word, and to present her to
> himself as a radiant church, without stain or
> wrinkle or any other blemish, *but holy and
> blameless.*[clxii]

The reason for the union of Christ and Church is our holiness,
and this holiness has nothing to do with dullness; it has
everything to do with love.

> As obedient children, do not conform to the evil
> desires you had when you lived in
> ignorance. But just as he who called you is holy,
> so be holy in all you do; for it is written: "Be

holy, because I am holy." Since you call on a Father who judges each person's work impartially, live out your time as foreigners here in reverent fear. For you know that it was not with perishable things such as silver or gold that you were redeemed from the empty way of life handed down to you from your ancestors, but with the precious blood of Christ, a lamb without blemish or defect. He was chosen before the creation of the world, but was revealed in these last times for your sake. Through him you believe in God, who raised him from the dead and glorified him, and so your faith and hope are in God._Now that you have purified yourselves by obeying the truth so that you have sincere love for each other, love one another deeply, from the heart.[clxiii]

Being "one flesh" with Christ means we are able to love because we have been made holy and pure inside; the cold stone heart has been changed into a warm fleshly heart that beats for others. And this has to mean married couples must exhibit the same kind of holy love towards their spouses. This is especially true when we realize the first humans were holy at their creation when humanity was declared to be "one flesh." As soon as sin entered, humans forgot all about their "one flesh"-ness and began to see other humans as disposable, as their enemies. Unsurprisingly, the story of Cain and Abel, the first fratricide recorded in the Bible, was one of envy and violence.[clxiv] Violence and deceit would continue to be the cardinal sins the prophets thundered against and the Law attempted to curb with the commands given to everyone to love God with their whole beings and their neighbor as themselves.

Incidentally, violence and deceit are also found in the letter to the Ephesians:

> Therefore each of you must put off falsehood and speak truthfully to your neighbor, for we are all members of one body. "In your anger do not sin": Do not let the sun go down while you are still angry, and do not give the devil a foothold. Anyone who has been stealing must steal no longer, but must work, doing something useful with their own hands, that they may have something to share with those in need. Do not let any unwholesome talk come out of your mouths, but only what is helpful for building others up according to their needs, that it may benefit those who listen. And do not grieve the Holy Spirit of God, with whom you were sealed for the day of redemption. Get rid of all bitterness, rage and anger, brawling and slander, along with every form of malice.[clxv]

Our tendency to be violent and deceitful is what love and holiness removes from us:

> That, however, is not the way of life you learned
> when you heard about Christ and were taught in

him in accordance with the truth that is in Jesus. You were taught, with regard to your former way of life, to put off your old self, which is being corrupted by its deceitful desires; to be made new in the attitude of your minds; and to put on the new self, created to be like God in true righteousness and holiness.[clxvi]

The above text is usually glossed over by the reader quickly for there doesn't seem to be anything interesting to capture anyone's attention, but if we pay just a little bit more attention, we'll see an incredible truth that makes the famous marriage passage sing an aria of sense. The holiness mentioned in Ephesians 5:21-33 is connected in this text to the "new self," created to be like God. This "new self," is what makes us one with Christ; the "old self" was what separated us from Christ due to the ignorance that caused us to do evil.[clxvii] The "new self" agrees with God; the "old self" agrees with something quite different, such as the King of Persia who had a proclamation sent out to all of his subjects concerning Queen Vashti.

> "Then Memukan replied in the presence of the king and the nobles, "Queen Vashti has done wrong, not only against the king but also against all the nobles and the peoples of all the provinces of King Xerxes. For the queen's conduct will become known to all the women, and so they will despise their husbands and say, 'King Xerxes commanded Queen Vashti to be

brought before him, but she would not come.'
This very day the Persian and Median women of
the nobility who have heard about the queen's
conduct will respond to all the king's nobles in
the same way. There will be no end of disrespect
and discord. Therefore, if it pleases the king, let
him issue a royal decree and let it be written in
the laws of Persia and Media, which cannot be
repealed, that Vashti is never again to enter the
presence of King Xerxes. Also let the king give
her royal position to someone else who is better
than she. Then when the king's edict is
proclaimed throughout all his vast realm, all the
women will respect their husbands, from the
least to the greatest." The king and his nobles
were pleased with this advice, so the king did as
Memukan proposed. He sent dispatches to all
parts of the kingdom, to each province in its own
script and to each people in their own language,
proclaiming that every man should be ruler over
his own household, using his native tongue.[clxviii]

The "old self" sees nothing wrong with such a proclamation,
but the "new self" has a new way of looking at things: the new
life lived in the Body of Christ that is no longer about having
authority over others, but about how we can and should rule
ourselves, because "the fruit of the Spirit is love, joy, peace,
forbearance, kindness, goodness, faithfulness, gentleness and
self-control" and "against such things there is no law."[clxix]

Since the woman and the man are equally holy, and there is no law against holy behavior, there is no need for authority in a Christian marriage as all authority was given because of sin.

Now that we know all of the above, let's go back to the idea that Ephesians and Colossians are twin letters. As already noted, in Ephesians the head-body relationship is explicitly connected to marriage, but in Colossians this connection is lacking.

> Wives, submit yourselves to your husbands, as is fitting in the Lord…. Husbands, love your wives and do not be harsh with them.[clxx]

The lack of the words "submit to one another" in Colossians has given the impression this submission is unilateral, but this view ignores the connection of submission to humility:

> Likewise, ye younger, submit yourselves unto the elder. Yea, all of you be subject one to another, and be clothed with humility: for God resisteth the proud, and giveth grace to the humble.[clxxi]

Humility is found in connection to mutual submission in both 1 Peter 5 and Ephesians 5, which makes it impossible for humility to appear in Colossians 3 without mutual submission being present in some form:

> Therefore, as God's chosen people, holy and dearly loved, clothe yourselves with compassion, kindness, humility, gentleness and patience. Bear with each other and forgive one another if any of you has a grievance against someone. Forgive as the Lord forgave you. And over all these virtues put on love, which binds them all together in perfect unity.[clxxii]

Since humility, love, holiness, and mutual submission are always found together, clearly they are meant for everyone, not just for some of us. All of these are necessary in order for us to do the one thing the Bible mentions explicitly when it talks about marriage: to please one's spouse.[clxxiii] And so we find that in the end, after all the patriarchal talk about power and authority and fussing about who does what and when, it all comes down to how we can best serve our spouses through love. And it is only fitting, as —

> "Love is patient, love is kind. It does not envy, it does not boast, it is not proud. It does not dishonor others, it is not self-seeking, it is not easily angered, it keeps no record of wrongs. Love does not delight in evil but rejoices with the truth. It always protects, always trusts, always hopes, always perseveres."[clxxiv]

Or, in the words of Edmund Spencer. "All for love, and nothing for reward." We are called to live a life of love as love drives out fear.[clxxv] Patriarchy wants us to be afraid of punishment, always looking for ways to please those in power. But love sets us free; free from fear, free from control. It sets us free to be who we are meant to be. And that is the one thing patriarchy cannot take away from us.

Chapter 10

Afterthoughts

"I may have been a victim of sexism throughout my upbringing,
But could have accepted it as part of my life."

Thoko Mpumlwana

We began this book with the idea women are people too, and together we've found that although people agree with this idea in general, a lot of people struggle with the concept of equal rights, and especially with women's rights as human rights. From philosophy to biology, politics, customs, and law, women have been viewed as inferior beings in need of the man's authority "for their own good." The most surprising element over the years has been women's own agreement with this assessment. Or, perhaps it shouldn't be such a surprise. As with most movements that seek to change things, people like to embrace the end results but distance themselves from the movement itself due to potential embarrassment; we want the rights to be there for us without having to fight for them. Especially women like the things feminism provides, such as the vote and right to wear what they want, college education and their own bank accounts. But at the same time they have a tendency to reject feminism as intrinsically evil and immoral—feminists are angry women who hate men, and what kind of woman wants to hate a man? Because of this negative stereotyping, feminism was relegated into the dark corners of academia right next to ancient philosophy sometime after the seventies, for as we have been told to ask ourselves, did Socrates or Steinem ever do anyone any good other than to stir trouble wherever they went? In the process of this distancing, the rights other people fought to give us became self-evident truths and no longer merited a conversation as to their origin. Why talk about feminism now that all the good things are here to stay? I'd say because rights are like relationships: here one day, gone the next, unless we pay attention. Or perhaps they are what our anatomy can never be—our true destiny.

Speaking of anatomy, if patriarchy is right and anatomy *is* destiny (i.e., women should have children because they have a womb), should they not also have ideas and independent thoughts because they have a mind? Isn't the brain with all of its synapses and grey matter part of the human anatomy too? Because the answer is such an obvious yes, one of the greatest insults patriarchy has thrown at women is this idea women's minds are somehow deficient, that women are just pretty little things with a lot of empty space in between their ears; that they are suited mostly for dull, repetitive jobs that no one else wants to do; that they should hide their intelligence, because in the end it's all about men and what they want, and they don't want smart women. And so the woman's womb became her destiny instead of her mind, and her body became the man's playground. Her dreams, wishes, and aspirations became the source of endless jokes for philosophers and comedians alike who wondered why women would ever want to do anything other than to cook and clean for the men in their lives.

But we do.

As a result of the persistent stereotype of the mindless woman, we find people regularly wondering why we spend so much of our common resources educating young women only to have them spend their days doing menial chores. This if of course ludicrous even in the eyes of patriarchy, which is why the education of girls is usually cut short in most patriarchal societies, and the only reason why western countries still keep on spending twelve to sixteen years educating their girls is because education is seen as a human right. But just because the patriarchal machine isn't able to prevent women from getting an education, it is still able to convince women to use their education as little as possible and this is where religious patriarchy gets to shine like a bright star in a dark night sky. It has done an absolutely superb job convincing women their "role" in life is homemaking; careers are for men by the order of God Almighty. But although the proof of the pudding may be in the eating, the proof of the joys of homemaking isn't in the doing. No matter how many days or years a woman spends in the home, nothing makes it more palatable or enjoyable; it's a rather depressing and monotonous way to spend one's days. And this begs the question, why would God design women to spend their days in such a way? The answer is as short as it is sweet — God didn't.

God gave women a mind and God expects them to use it. No matter how much patriarchy claims women's brains aren't as evolved as men's brains, perhaps if men spent less time fighting women who try to use theirs they would find their argument misguided, and quite honestly, foolish. If women were truly less intelligent than men, all we would have to do is have men and women take the same test and watch the women fail every time, the way they fail if they were to compete against men at sports events due to their lesser physical strength. But instead of failing, millions of girls, and young (and not so young) women compete in the intellectual realm every day and thrive. And perhaps this is the true cause of all the annoyance as the man's much vaunted reason has been the source of the man's rule for a long time now. All of this begs naturally the question, if men and women are equally intelligent, why should a woman be restricted to a life in the domestic sphere if she has the intelligence and ability to send a space shuttle to the moon?[clxxvi]

Yes, why indeed.

Words have meaning, and as humans we build our lives around words and concepts as seen in Descartes famous dictum, "I think, therefore I am." Because words affect our minds either in a positive or a negative way, a lot of words are designed to make us feel insignificant and small. As women we are told we aren't smart enough, good enough, worthy enough. When we absorb negative words, they become a permanent part of who we are, and we begin to act accordingly. To combat the effect of negative words, we need to hear lots of positive, loving, and affirming words (we need to hear at least three times more positive words than negative words).[clxxvii] We need to hear we are capable, strong, and worthy, and we need to hear those words often; just as it takes only a split second to create a stain, the washing machine takes an hour to get rid of the stain. It's why empowering ourselves with positive words is so important and why patriarchy insists on a very different message. In fact, hearing we are important and valuable is even more important than giving women equal opportunities, for without the impact of positive words women are less likely to use those opportunities. Instead, they use their words to convince *other* women they aren't worthy and should accept a man's authority. Patriarchy divides women in order to conquer them, but feminism teaches women to create strong bonds of sisterhood; we need less Cinderella stories, more affirming stories — our own stories.

Patriarchy considers subjection to be benign and for the benefit of the one being subjected, but subjection that doesn't allow you to be who you truly are; doesn't allow you to follow your own intuition, your gut reaction, your own wisdom and knowledge, is far from benign. And although this kind of subjection may exclude bodily harm, it is harmful to the mind as it forces the mind to accept something it would otherwise reject. Feminism frees, not just women, but all of us from the need to control others. Yet, although feminism benefits everyone, it can only be experienced by women, as only women need to affirm their own humanity in a patriarchal world that denies women's humanity in a thousand ways every day. As women we shouldn't be afraid to embrace feminism. We need feminism to know and understand that we are primarily humans and secondarily women, just as we are primarily human and secondarily rich/ poor/ white/ brown/ black/ red/ yellow/ tall/ short/ clumsy/ brilliant/ lovely/ gentle/ kind. It may seem self-evident, but think of all the little things that have happened in your life, the thinly veiled insults, the disrespect, the catcalling, the lost promotions, the inflated mechanic bills, the time you were told to mind your own business and go back to the kitchen, all the moments when you wished you were a boy instead of a girl. By now you may be so used to it you hardly notice any of it, or you may be seething with rage. No matter what your feelings, feminism is for you, for you have a right to receive equal respect, *real* respect. A woman is not a doll, or a drudge, or an object. A woman is a human being and therefore worthy of the same respect all humans merit just by the virtue of their own humanity. Women belong to the human race, not to something above or below, for we don't consort with devils or sing with the angels, nor are our faces frozen works of art that should not be sullied with real thoughts and feelings. We don't belong in the artless world of platitudes and mindless conversation, a world void of real and true conversation. We don't belong in the boredom of the home void of the company of other grownups, in the endless hamster wheel of housework. We *do* belong in the places of business, education, and finance. We *do* belong behind the pulpit, behind the bench, behind the counter. We belong everywhere the man has always been, but this is exactly the problem: if men would allow us to occupy their space, they would have to occupy ours, and that's not something they are willing to do quite yet;

the dishes do still seem to stack too high for the male ego. Women (and slaves) are the global mess cleaners, the ones who spend their days tidying, washing and scrubbing everything that is dirty, while children and men make the messes. No wonder then that so many philosophers and theologians have been obsessed with the ideas of purity as there is something in us that resists the idea of cleanliness. But just as with our modern obsession of cleaning everything, our "wise men" have had a tendency to go overboard until everything became dirty: sex, bodies, women, words, thoughts. They had to be sanitized until there was nothing left other than the hollow shell of a life void of passions and feeling. In order to express forbidden feelings and thoughts, people had to hide in the shadows and deny them in the open. It created a society ruled by lies and deceit, and because of it, one of the goals and aims of feminism has been to reduce the deceit by reducing the items that are considered dirty. Sex was a top priority because of what the perception of sex as dirty does to women: when sex is dirty, a woman who wants and enjoys sex becomes herself dirty and therefore worthy of less respect, much like the *infamia* of old Rome. Men are still allowed to enjoy sex, but not too much, for a man who appears unable to control his passions in the realm of sex cannot be trusted to control himself in any other matter, especially if he is easily swayed by the beauty of a woman. But what are we saying here, really? Aren't we saying feminism has a wonderful ability to cut through all the hypocrisy and deceit and lies and get us to behave like real human beings, the way we were meant to live and be? And this leads us to the next question, why would anyone want anything different?

Theologically speaking, the reason patriarchy has lasted this long is its ability to feed our "lower nature," that part of us that is egotistical and seeks only to gratify our selfish feelings and thoughts. Patriarchy has no love, and because it has no love, it has no ability to see other human beings as worthy of love and respect. We all struggle with this, men and women alike, and it is as universal as the daily sunrise, but the cure isn't *more* patriarchy; patriarchy has no answers, it comes with only more problems. The only cure to the problems created by patriarchy is equality. Change begins with the recognition there is a better way of doing things, one that includes all of us instead of just the few of us who desire to rule the rest, citing equity. We need to safeguard everyone's rights and freedoms, and that to do so we need to ensure that our laws, customs, and institutions are impartial and work for everyone. We need to change how we speak about humans. In other words, we need to re-write our collective narrative.

Our humanity is what patriarchy denies when it restricts our movements and aspirations, and demands we obey men. Yet, feminism isn't an ideology that can be used to force others to conform.[clxxviii] It is not a set of beliefs or behaviors intended to set a moral standard for everyone to follow. Feminism is for you and me, because subjection is a mindset. It's not outside of us. It's inside us, in our minds; *we* believe others have the right to tell us what to do, and *we* obey. Some men (and some women) rightly complain about being forced to adopt feminism. No one can be forced to accept feminism—but neither can anyone be forced to accept patriarchy. If a man truly wants to find a woman who will obey him, no one can prevent him; if a woman truly wants to be free, she cannot be stopped. The rejection of conformity is not about feminism or patriarchy; it's about justice. Justice requires we refrain from causing harm and actively seek to prevent situations that cause harm, and this means we must let others live in accordance to their own beliefs. Although we should all be free to live according to our own values, too much personal freedom takes away from the freedom of others. It isn't enough to allow everybody be who they are if they cannot be who they wish to be because of oppressive laws and customs others were free to create.[clxxix]

In our eagerness to free ourselves from patriarchy, we have tried to put the cart before the horse: we have tried to create a just world through feminism and free ourselves through other ideologies. Although finding faith can be one of the most freeing experiences a human can experience, the purpose of faith is not to free us as women. The purpose of faith is to make us into just people, and justice has to do with how we treat each other. Feminism cannot create a just world because feminism is about you and me as women, about our humanity, not about how we treat other people. In other words, feminism isn't the antibiotics or the fix-all cure that heals all the ills of the world; every ill needs its own remedy. When we begin to attach distinctions to feminism, however insignificant in our eyes, it begins to resemble patriarchy and suddenly feminism becomes just another excuse for the oppression of women. To put it succinctly, there has never been nor can there ever be such a thing as white feminism; it's as impossible as wealth feminism. Some feminists are racist, others are classicists, but none of them deny other women's humanity based on these categories. Our societies are filled with multiple layers, and women aren't immune to this kind of thinking. In fact, the more patriarchal the society, the more everybody grows up absorbing and accepting discriminatory ideas and behavior patterns. We need to fight racism and classicism, but we must do so as free humans, having realized our humanity through feminism. We can't fight racism as feminists as racism doesn't deny women's humanity; racism denies the humanity of people based on their ethnicity. We must fight racism by affirming the humanity of all of those who have had their humanity questioned by racist policies just as we fight sexism by affirming women's humanity. Any other arrangement is just another form of paternalistic patriarchy.

And so we end this book with the affirmation every woman needs feminism. As women we need to learn to love ourselves, appreciate our bodies, celebrate our minds, and understand that being a woman is not a shameful thing, it's a creative thing. Dr. Wayne Dyer has the following advice to offer and I hope you will take it with you:

> After all, what could be better than the freedom of going through life without feeling that people and circumstances control you without your permission.[clxxx]

Patriarchy insists control is love, but what kind of love demands you renounce yourself? As women we are all worthy of a life that is uniquely our own, and we all hold in ourselves the power to create not only a new life, but a beautiful life when we free ourselves through feminism. But we cannot stop there. As free humans we need to work towards the liberation of all humans. Until every human is free, no human is truly free.

Live free, love freely.

This is the message of the Final Wave.

This book is written with gratitude to all women
Who dared to create waves
Refused to be silenced
Who stood up for their right to be human

Thank You

Endnotes

[i] Saudi women cast the ballot for the first time in 2015.

[ii] I would write about how patriarchy has influenced all religions and how to dismantle all religious patriarchy, but since I don't have the necessary knowledge, religious patriarchy in this book refers solely to Christian patriarchal theology.

[iii] The system wouldn't be called *patriarches* — the rule of the fathers — if the fathers, i.e., men, didn't rule.

[iv] Annie Bunting, Benjamin N. Lawrance, Richard L. Roberts, ed. *Marriage by Force?* [Ohio University Press, 2016] 16.

[v] Genesis 2:18

[vi] Augustine, *Of the Works of Monks*

[vii] Genesis 1:26-27

[viii] Jonathan Haidt, *The Righteous Mind: Why Good People Are Divided by Politics and Religion* [NY: Random House 2012] 25.

[ix] Ibid., 45

[x] Matthew 7:1

[xi] John 8:2-11

[xii] Genesis 1:26-27, Romans 3

[xiii] "The more that consciousness is influenced by prejudices, errors, fantasies, and infantile wishes, the more the already existing gap will widen into a neurotic
dissociation and lead to a more or less artificial life, far removed from healthy instincts, nature, and truth" (Carl G Jung, *Man and his Symbols* [London: Aldus Books Limited, 1964] 49.

[xiv] I must hasten to add here that having a bias is in itself not necessarily a bad thing as biases allow us to make quick decisions, but they hide also prejudices and the more we believe ourselves to be free from biases the more biased we become.

[xv] *On Christian Doctrine*, Book III, Ch 17.25

[xvi] Miriam Gurko, *The Ladies of Seneca Falls: The Birth of the Woman's Rights Movement* [NY: Shocken Books, 1974] 130.

[xvii] Barbara Welter, "*The Cult of True Womanhood*: 1820-1860" (1966) http://www.colorado.edu/AmStudies/lewis/1025/cultwoman.pdf [Accessed 10/31/2016].

[xviii] "Decades before Kinsey, Stanford professor Clelia Mosher polled Victorian-era women on their bedroom behavior — then kept the startling results under wraps…. Indeed, many of the surveyed women were

decidedly unshrinking. One, born in 1844, called sex "a normal desire" and observed that "a rational use of it tends to keep people healthier." Offered another, born in 1862, "The highest devotion is based upon it, a very beautiful thing, and I am glad nature gave it to us…. So if not all Victorian women scorned sex, why do we think of them as prudish? First, says Freedman, the notion of passionlessness wasn't universal, it was a class privilege, a way for wealthier women to claim respectability that more sexually vulnerable slave, immigrant and working-class women couldn't. "To some extent it's a protection of women from the sense of availability, and in other ways it's a limitation on them and denying their sexuality," Freedman says. Virtue was also a way for women to demonstrate good citizenship — men expressed this in the public sphere, and women in the home"(http://alumni.stanford.edu/get/page/magazine/article/?article_id=29954)[Accessed 12/01/2016].

xix This myth tells us also that women should be divided into subsections based on color, which is why the first wave feminists were predominantly white. It is a horrible injustice that third and fourth waves have fought hard to rectify. We are all women, and therefore human, regardless of the color of our skin.

xx Friedrich Nietzsche described this as "Will to Power" in his book, *Beyond Good and Evil;* one of the most honest philosophical explorations of human aspiration to gain power.

xxi "Lewis et al. (1976) consider that unhealthy mythology is used to cloud and distort reality. Healthy myths, they contend, fill in gaps of observation and provide a matrix of shared meaning. What is more they are not rigid but can be changed. They are gentle and humorous, thus allowing for human frailty and not demanding that people live up to (or down to) stereotyped images" (Journal of Family Therapy (1 979) 1 : 103-1 16 *Re-editing family mythology during family therapy* by John Byng-Hall).

xxii Barbara Ehrenreich, *For her Own Good: Two Centuries of the Expert Advice to Women* [NY:Anchor, 2013]

xxiii *The Ladies of Seneca Falls,* 127-128.

xxiv Lee Holcombe, Wives and Property: *Reform of the Married Woman's Property Law in Nineteenth-Century England* [University of Toronto Press, Canada, 1983] 14.

xxv To the outside world, the wife was known as "Mrs. [insert husband's name]" as she had no separate legal existence. Modern women who still relish the title "Mrs." forget its origin and the severe legal disabilities that were associated with coverture.

xxvi *Wives and Property,* 35.

xxvii Ibid., 4

xxviii Claudia Zaher: *When a Woman's Marital Status Determined Her Legal*

Status: A Research Guide on the Common Law Doctrine of Coverture
(http://people.virginia.edu/~jdk3t/ZaherWMS.pdf) [Accessed 10/7/16].
xxix As explored elsewhere in great detail, Genesis 3:16 has been changed
numerous times to accommodate changes to patriarchal theology. See
"Genesis 3: The Origin of Gender Roles"; "When Dogmas Die: The Return
of Biblical Equality"; "Recovering From Un-Biblical Manhood and
Womanhood: A Response to Evangelical Patriarchy."
xxx *The Ladies of Seneca Falls*, 124.
xxxi *Wives and Property*, 8.
xxxii Rosa Parks was chosen to represent the de-segregation efforts of the
public transit system in Montgomery, Alabama, due to her respectability.
xxxiii "The happy idea of using a proletarian holiday celebration as a means
to attain the eight-hour day was first born in Australia. The workers there
decided in 1856 to organize a day of complete stoppage together with
meetings and entertainment as a demonstration in favor of the eight-hour
day. The day of this celebration was to be April 21. At first, the Australian
workers intended this only for the year 1856. But this first celebration had
such a strong effect on the proletarian masses of Australia, enlivening them
and leading to new agitation, that it was decided to repeat the celebration
every year.... Thus, the idea of a proletarian celebration was quickly
accepted and, from Australia, began to spread to other countries until
finally it had conquered the whole proletarian world" (Rosa Luxemburg,
What are the Origins of May Day? 1894).
xxxiv The downside of financial independence is the dissolution of tightknit
communities as humanity hasn't quite yet figured out how to create
communities without some measure of coercion. The problem with this
coercion is that it is usually directed toward women as patriarchy views
women as responsible for the creation and maintenance of communities.
Elizabeth Cady Stanton saw this truth clearly as she wrote, "While man
enjoys all the rights, he preaches all the duties to a woman."
xxxv "Slaveholders in the British North American colonies became
increasingly fearful that Christianization of slaves would lead to demands
for emancipation. In 1667 Virginia passed a law declaring that conversion
did not change the status of a person from slave to free. Other colonies
passed similar laws during the seventeenth and early eighteenth centuries"
(*The Slave Experience: Religion* by Kimberly Sambol-Tosco
http://www.pbs.org/wnet/slavery/ experience/religion/history.html)
[Accessed 1/8/2017].
xxxvi Ephesians 4:15-16
xxxvii https://spiritualsoundingboard.com/category/organizations-

movements/doug-phillips-vision-forum/[Accessed 1/7/2017].

xxxviii 1 Timothy 2:11 is cited as support.

xxxix Jung described this kind of extreme "understanding" as a very real possibility even in psychoanalysis unless care is taken: "Subjectivation (in technical terms, transference and countertransference) creates isolation from the environment, a social limitation which neither party wishes for but which invariably sets in when understanding predominates and is no longer balanced by knowledge. As understanding deepens, the further removed it becomes from knowledge. An ideal understanding would ultimately result in each party's unthinkingly going along with the other's experience — a state of uncritical passivity coupled with the most complete subjectivity and lack of social responsibility. Understanding carried to such lengths us in any case impossible, for it would require the virtual identification of two different individuals. Sooner or later the relationship reaches a point where one partner feels his being forced to sacrifice his own individuality so that it may be assimilated by that of the other. This inevitable consequence breaks the understanding, for understanding also presupposes the integral preservation of the individuality of both partners. It is therefore advisable to carry understanding only to the point where the balance between understanding and knowledge is reached, for understanding at all costs is injurious to both partners" (C G Jung, *The Undiscovered Self with Symbols and the Interpretation of Dreams* [NJ: Princeton University Press, 1990] 29).

xl William Blackstone. *Commentaries on the Laws of England*. Vol, 1 (1765), pages 442-445, (emphasis added).

xli Theologically speaking, against the infantilizing of women stands the purpose of the existence of pastors, teachers, prophets and evangelists in the church as outlined in Ephesians 4:11-13: the maturity of the body of Christ, that has as its explicit purpose the training of each member for the work of ministry; there is no gender barrier mentioned in the text.

xlii *Nicomachean Ethics*, 1130a1-10

xliii Aristotle, *Politics*, 1259a10, 1260a30

xliv *The Family in Political Thought*, 45.

xlv Jean Bethke Elsthain, *The Family in Political Thought* [MA: University of Massachusetts Press, 1982] 157-159.

xlvi John Stuart Mill, *The Subjection of Women*; original Printing by London, Longmans, Green, Reader, and Dyer, 1869 [NY: reprinted by Source Book Press, 1970] 51.

xlvii Beverly Zink-Sawyer, *Preachers to Suffragists: Woman's Rights and Religious Conviction in the Lives of three Nineteenth-Century American Clergywomen* [KY: Westminster John Knox Press, 2003] 116.

xlviii Peregrine Bingham, A.B., *The Law of Infancy and Coverture* [Burlington,

1849] 182-183.

[xlix] Ibid.

[l] Ibid.

[li] L.H Butterfield, ed et al. *The Book of Abigail and John* [Harvard University Press, 1975] 120, 127.

[lii] https://www.whitehouse.gov/about-the-white-house/presidents/john-adams/

[liii] Ibid., 156

[liv] "As Homer says: "Each gives law to his children and his wives." (Aristotle, *Politics*, 1252b20).

[lv] *Politics* 1252a20-1252b10

[lvi] *Aristotle, Politics* 1253b5-10, 1254a15-25

[lvii] *Ethics, 11131,1-10*

[lviii] Diogenes *Laertius* III, 46 https://etudesplatoniciennes.revues.org/ 277# tocto1n3 (emphasis added) [Accessed 11/03/2016].

[lix] George C. Williams, *Sex and Evolution* (Princeton, NJ: Princeton University Press, 1977) 43-44.

[lx] Ibid., 40-41

[lxi] Ursula King ed., *Feminist Theology from the Third World* [NY: Orbis Books, 1996] 256.

[lxii] "Hesiod was perhaps the first to tell the story we have just read of the woman who, like Eve, was said to be the source of all human misery. Angry at Prometheus for having stolen fire from the gods to give to humanity, Zeus decides to punish the human species by creating one of the earliest examples of archetypal femme fatale. It has been suggested by Jane Harrison (Prolegomenona to the Study of Greek Religion, pp 284-85) that this myth is a patriarchal perversion of a story that must originally have reflected the meaning of Pandora's name, the "All-Giver," a title that also belonged to the Earth Goddess, Rhea, and suggest that Pandora was in reality an earth goddess as well. Here the myth is rewritten by Charlene Spretnak and Pandora's earlier nature restored to her" (David Adams Leeming, *The World of Myth, an Anthology,* [NY: Oxford University Press, 1990] 177-178).

[lxiii] 1 Timothy 2:14; 2 Corinthians 11:3

[lxiv] John 7:53–8:11

[lxv] Nancy Chodorow, *Reproduction of Mothering: Psychoanalysis and the Sociology of Gender* [University of California Press, 1978] 51.

[lxvi] Ibid., 89

[lxvii] Ibid., 29

[lxviii] Ibid., 185

[lxix] Ibid., 74

[lxx] Ibid., 29

lxxi Ibid., 30,32

lxxii This is perhaps one of the greatest reasons religious patriarchy is so against evolution as it reveals the patriarchal bias behind its theology.

lxxiii Ambrose, *Three Books Concerning Virgins,* Book I, Ch 3, 11.

lxxiv Ibid., Book II, Ch VI, 31

lxxv *"Why should I further speak of the painful ministrations and services due to their husbands from wives, to whom before slaves God gave the command to serve? ☐"* (*Three Books Concerning Virgins* Book I, Ch VI, 26.27) Ambrose is referring to the belief that God punished Eve with subjection to Adam due to her rebellion. Genesis 3:16 was believed to affirm this belief.

lxxvi Book 3, ch VII, 32-37

lxxvii Thomas Aquinas, *Summa Theologica*, First Part, Question 92, Objection 1

lxxviii Ibid., Question 92, Answer to Objection 2

lxxix George Lakoff, *Moral Politics* [IL: The University of Chicago Press, 1996] 67-107.

lxxx Even if patriarchy was right in saying strength is a masculine virtue, it wouldn't mean that only *men* have strength, for masculinity and maleness are not the same thing, nor can femininity and femaleness be treated as equivalents as masculinity and femininity are cultural constructs and differ greatly around the world.

lxxxi In modern language submission equals obedience. This was, however, not the case in the ancient world, where submission meant cooperation between equals as contrasted to obedience that was owed to a superior.

lxxxii Columbus Salley, Ronald Behm, *Your God is Too White*, [IL: Inter-Varsity Press, 1970] 22.

lxxxiii Eva Cantarella, *Pandora's Daughters: The Role and Status of Women in Greek and Roman Antiquity (Ancient Society and History)* [MD: John Hopkins University Press, 1987] 33.

lxxxiv As with all human relationships, there are three levels of politeness: formality, deference, and friendship Formality removes emotions (which is why formality is always connected to authority), deference skirts the issue and gives options (but not enough to cause trouble), and friendship prohibits insults. But there is also a fourth level of politeness: empty platitudes. When people have nothing to say, they speak of the weather, or shoes, or dogs, anything that doesn't challenge. Whereas silence would be considered rude, and talking about real issues isn't possible, talking about nothingness fills the void (See: Robin Lakoff, *Language and Woman's Place* [NY: Harper & Row, 1975] 65).

lxxxv *Politics*, 1260a30

lxxxvi *Politics*, 1255a35-1255b5

lxxxvii Philippe Aries and George Duby, ed. *A History of Private Life: From Pagan Rome to Byzantium* [MA: Harvard University Press, 1987] 119.

lxxxviii *Politics*, 1253b30

lxxxix His argument rests on the premise that the feebleminded and mentally disabled were suited to a life of slavery, as they needed someone to care for them being unable to care for themselves.

xc *The Ladies of Seneca Falls*, 129.

xci From the diary of Lucretia Mott: "Evening. Several sent to us to persuade us not to offer ourselves to the Convention--Colver [Rev. Nathaniel Colver, pastor of the First Free baptist Church in Boston and a delegate of the

National Baptist Anti Slavery Convention] rather bold in his suggestions-- answered and of course offended him. W. Morgan and Scales informed us "it wasn't designed as a *World* Convention--that was mere Poetical license," and that all power would rest with the "London Committee of Arrangements." Prescod of Jamaica (colored) thought it would lower the dignity of the Convention and bring ridicule on the whole thing if ladies were admitted--he was told that similar reasons were urged in Philadelphia for the exclusion of colored people from our meetings--but had we yielded on such flimsy arguments, we might as well have abandoned our enterprise. Colver thought Women constitutionally unfit for public or business meetings--he was told that the colored man too was said to be *constitutionally* unfit to mingle with the white man. He left the room angry"

(http://www.wwhp.org/Resources/Slavery/mottdiary1840.html)[Access ed 1/13/2017].

xcii These articles appeared as part of "Appendix — Chapter IV" of History of Woman's Suffrage by Elizabeth Cady Stanton and others ©1999 Stephen Railton & the University of Virginia

(http://utc.iath.virginia.edu/abolitn/abwmbt.html) [Accessed 1/30/2017].

xciii Simone de Beauvoir, *The Second Sex* [NY: Vintage Books, 2011] 3-4.

xciv *Metaphysics* 1018a5-1018b5

xcv http://history

world.org/Civilization,%20women_in_patriarchal_societies.htm [Accessed 10/1/2016].

xcvi William Shakespeare, *The Taming of the Shrew*, II.i.261–272, V.ii.140– 183

xcvii *Epigrams*

xcviii Elizabeth Janeway, *Man's World, Woman's Place: A Study in Social Mythology* [NY: Morrow, 1971] 105.

xcix Arthur Schopenhauer, *Über die Weiber*

^c bell hooks, *killing rage* [NY: Holt, 1995] 138.

^{ci} Argument Against Women's Suffrage, 1911. Prepared by J. B. Sanford, Chairmen of Democratic Caucus.

^{cii} Augustine, *On the Trinity,* In Fifteen Books, Book XII, Ch. 7.

^{ciii} *A History of Private Life*, 248.

^{civ} Plato, *Phaedo* 81a-e

^{cv} *Preachers to Suffragists*, 128.

^{cvi} Romans 5, 1 Tim 2:4

^{cvii} Gustavo Gutierrez, *A Theology of Liberation: History, Politics, and Salvation* [NY: Orbis, 1973] xxiv.

^{cviii} *The Undiscovered Self*, 28.

^{cix} Emily Zakin, *"Psychoanalytic Feminism,"* The Stanford Encyclopedia of Philosophy, Summer 2011 Edition http://plato.stanford.edu/archives/ sum2011/entries/feminism-psychoanalysis/ [Accessed 10/7/2016].

^{cx} Plato rejected the patriarchal nuclear family, because he believed it to be the cause of all the arguments about children and inheritance rights within the community. The more children, the more resources were needed, and with expansion came a greater risk of war with the neighboring cities.

^{cxi} *Totem and Taboo, 21-25.*

^{cxii} As Anselm of Canterbury observed, it is our reason that lies to us (*On Truth*, 6).

^{cxiii} "The three elements, (1) the inheritance of acquired characteristics, (2) the repetition over many generation, and (3) the application to the physiological that we find in Darwin's Variation, are present in Freud's formulation in the Ego and the Id of the formation of the superego: "The experiences of the ego... when they have been repeated often enough and with sufficient strength in many individuals in successive generations, transform themselves, so to say, into experiences of the id, the impressions of which are preserved by heredity. Thus in the id, which is capable of being inherited, are harboured residues of the existence of countless egos; and when the ego forms its super-ego out of the id, it may perhaps only be reviving shapes of former egos and bringing them to resurrection" (1923, SE 19:38) (Lucille B. Ritvo, *Darwin's Influence on Freud: A Tale of Two Sciences* [CT: Yale University Press, 1992] 68).

^{cxiv} Sigmund Freud, *Femininity*

^{cxv} Ibid.

^{cxvi} *The Undiscovered Self*, 5.

^{cxvii} Mary Wollstonecraft, *A Vindication of the rights of Woman*, Second Edition, 1792 London Edition [W.W Norton & Company, 1975] 7.

^{cxviii} Ibid., 95

^{cxix} 1 Samuel 25; Matthew 14:1-12

^{cxx} Arthur Schopenhauer, *Über die Weiber*

cxxi Sarah B. Pomeroy, *Goddesses, Whores, Wives and Slaves* (New York: Shocken Books, 1995), 150.

cxxii Chrysostom, *Homilies on First Timothy*, Homily IX.

cxxiii Rosalind Rosenberg, *Beyond Separate Spheres: Intellectual Roots of Modern Feminism* (CT: Yale University Press, 1982), 5-6.

cxxiv Edith Deen, *The Bible's Legacy For Womanhood* [A Spire Books, New Jersey, 1976] 117.

cxxv Eve S. Buzawa, Carl G. Buzawa, *Domestic Violence: The Criminal Justice Response* [CA: Sage Publications, 2003] 60.

cxxvi Tertullian, *On the Apparel of Women*, Book I, Ch. I.

cxxvii Peter Adamson, *Philosophy In the Hellenistic & Roman World*: *A History of Philosophy Without Any Gaps* [Oxford University Press, 2015] 226.

cxxviii Anne Llewellyn Barstow, *Witchcraze: A New History of The European Witch Hunts* [CA: Pandora, 1994] 103-104.

cxxix Joe Scarborough wrote a tweet about Hillary Clinton's conspicuously lacking smile during the 2016 presidential primaries: "Smile. You just had a big night. #Primary Day"http://www.theguardian.com/commentisfree /2016 /mar/17/hillary-clinton-facing-sexism-sexist-politics [Accessed 11/01/2016].

cxxx Read more at EBONY http://www.ebony.com/news-views/when-i-stopped-asking-women-to-smile-981#ixzz43DLTKTtP[Accessed 10/15/2016].

cxxxi Ephesians 2:14-18, 3:6

cxxxii *The Undiscovered Self*, 35.

cxxxiii As Tacitus had noted, polygamy was customary among some of these northern "barbarians". And an old moral principle, enunciated by St Augustine in the *Reply to Faustus*, could very well have been invoked: "…A plurality of wives was no crime when it was the custom; and it is a crime now because it is no longer the custom." Augustine's argument was that the practice of polygamy becomes wrong when it is no longer customary; because, then, it arises only from an "excess of lust."(Franz Böckle, *The Future of Marriage as Institution* [NY: Herder and Herder, 1970] 33).

cxxxiv *The Future of Marriage Das Institution*, 31-32.

cxxxv *Mothering and Psychoanalysis*, 36.

cxxxvi *A History of Private Life*, 261.

cxxxvii Lawrence G. Wrenn, ed, *Divorce and Remarriage in the Catholic Church* [NY: The Missionary Society of St. Paul the Apostle, 1973] 74-75.

cxxxviii As consent became far more important than the contract, Scandinavian countries amended the ceremony by having the bride and groom walk down the aisle together as a sign of their mutual consent to get married.

cxxxix David G. Hunter, PhD, *Sex, Sin and Salvation: What Augustine Really*

Said (lecture text) http://www.jknirp.com/aug3.htm [Accessed 09/15/2016].

cxl *A History of Private Life*, 254.

cxli Susan C. Seymour, *Women, Family, and Child Care in India: A World in Transition* [Cambridge, 1999] 269-270.

cxlii *Divorce and Remarriage in the Catholic Church*, 19-20.

cxliii Jeremiah 3:8

cxliv Ephesians 5:5

cxlv James 4:1-4

cxlvi Colossians 2:18-19, emphasis added.

cxlvii Philippians 2:3-4

cxlviii 1 John 4:20

cxlix Philippians 2

cl 1 John 4:8

cli *Divorce and Remarriage in the Catholic Church*, 147.

clii Ephesians 5:1-2, John 15:9-17

cliii Ephesians 5:22-33

cliv 1 Corinthians 12

clv Ephesians 4:2-3, 4:32-5:1-2,25

clvi Mark 10:5-9

clvii Genesis 2:20-24

clviii 2 Samuel 19:11-12, KJV

clix See also Gen 29:14-15, Judges 9:1-2, 2 Samuel 5:1-2, 1 Chronicles 11:1

clx "Neither may we take the "one flesh" reference as proof of divinely established monogamous order. The two that become one, though in the singular, applies to all men and women" (*The Future of Marriage as Institution*, 8).

clxi Ephesians 5:28-33

clxii Ephesians 5:25-27 (emphasis added)

clxiii 1 Peter 1:14-22 (emphasis added)

clxiv Genesis 4

clxv Ephesians 4:25-3

clxvi Ephesians 4:20-24

clxvii Ephesians 4:17-19

clxviii Esther 1:16-22; Some have tried to get around the obvious meaning of the text by saying Queen Vashti was told to appear without clothing, but the conclusion is not supported by the text itself that simply states that she refused to leave the *harem* to appear before the King (a similar crime was daring to appear before the King without having been summoned) and that her example would have given other women the courage to act in a similar manner.

clxix Galatians 5:22-24

clxx Colossians 3:18-19

clxxi 1 Peter 5:5 KJV

clxxii Colossians 3:12-14

clxxiii "But I want you to be free from concern. One who is unmarried is concerned about the things of the Lord, how he may please the Lord; but one who is married is concerned about the things of the world, how he may please his wife, and *his*
interests are divided. The woman who is unmarried, and the virgin, is concerned about the things of the Lord, that she may be holy both in body and spirit; but one who is married is concerned about the things of the world, how she may please her husband. This I say for your own benefit; not to put a restraint upon you, but to promote what is appropriate and *to secure* undistracted devotion to the Lord" (1 Corinthians 7:32-35).

clxxiv 1 Corinthians 13:4-7

clxxv 1 John 4:18

clxxvi "As a computer, she calculated the trajectory for Alan Shepard, the first American in space. Even after NASA began using electronic computers, John Glenn requested that she personally recheck the calculations made by the new electronic computers before his flight aboard Friendship 7 – the mission on which he became the first American to orbit the Earth. She continued to work at NASA until 1986 combining her math talent with electronic computer skills. Her calculations proved as critical to the success of the Apollo Moon landing program and the start of the Space Shuttle program, as they did to those first steps on the country's journey into space." (Katherine Johnson: *The Girl Who Loved to Count.* https://www.nasa.gov/feature/katherine-johnson-the-girl-who-loved-to-count)[Accessed 12/30/2016].

clxxvii https://www.psychologytoday.com/blog/words-can-change-your-brain/201208/the-most-dangerous-word-in-the-world [Accessed 12/15/2016]

clxxviii Although I speak of feminism as something that is for women, I recognize that feminism is beneficial for both men and women, just as patriarchy "works" for both men and women.

clxxix Freedom without love creates the illusion that we are free to ignore others.

clxxx Dr. Wayne W. Dyer, *Change Your Thoughts – Change Your Life: Living the Wisdom of the Tao* [Hay House, 2007] 123.

www.ingramcontent.com/pod-product-compliance
Lightning Source LLC
Chambersburg PA
CBHW062140280526
45788CB00001B/240